A Year in Bloom

A Year in Bloom

Flowering Bulbs for Every Season

Lucy Bellamy

Photography by
Jason Ingram

Introduction

I love bulbs. I like them for their optimism, their resilience, and for their transient beauty. I like the forms and colours of their flowers at every stage of their opening and, whenever I see a bulb in full flower, I am sure, in that moment, that it is my favourite. I am not alone in this. From commonsensical Margery Fish, who naturalized *Galanthus* in 'The Ditch' in her garden at East Lambrook Manor in Somerset, to Anna Pavord with her passion for the tulip that drove men mad, to artist Cedric Morris, who deliberately crossed and raised thousands of iris seedlings in search of particular markings, and the gardeners who cultivate and conserve rare and historic tulip varieties in serried and glorious ranks at Hortus Bulborum in the Netherlands for us to enjoy, there are many who share my enthusiasm.

Learning how a bulb lives its life reveals that there is also pleasure for the gardener in its process. 'True' bulbs – and their close relatives corms, tubers and rhizomes, which are often described by the umbrella term 'bulb' – are dormant underground shoots or stems, wrapped in a brown papery package that contains everything they need to grow into a wonderful flower. They have adapted to leapfrog seasons and remain underground during cold or drought, ready to be pulled up to the light as soon as environmental conditions are in their favour.

In the lexicon of bulbs, 'spring' is the buzzword for many, synonymous with flashes of yellow daffodils and home to the tulip. The appeal of spring bulbs is twofold: the timing of their flowering marks the end of the winter and the start of all good things to come – 'Remember, though, they cannot cancel spring,' wrote artist David Hockney in his uplifting manifesto about art, and the same is true of spring bulbs. Secondly, bulbs that flower in spring are planted in autumn, offering an opportunity, in the mind's eye at least, to skip over the winter months and steal a march on the seasons. To dismiss summer, autumn and winter, however, is to miss out on the joys and plea-sures of a bulb-rich year, which starts with small flowers such as snowdrops and squills, stirred into life by the onset of wet weather, and ends with the giant-flowered *Hippeastrum*.

However, with so many varieties to choose from, how are we to select the best? Which is the most covetable snowdrop? Which daffodils grow in grass? Which tulips are reliably perennial? Which fritillary is best for bees? It is the mark of a true plantsperson to seek out only the best cultivars of the best plants and, in my work, I am lucky to be able to call upon the expertise of the most visionary contemporary gardeners – international garden designers, landscape architects and forward-thinking head gardeners who grow and observe bulbs every day. In this book are their recommendations.

Finding out who selected what and why is fascinating and revealing. Landscape architects and garden designers tended towards firmly estab-lished favourites, albeit in new and inspiring combinations. Almost as important as the bulb itself was how it was used – its numbers, companions and location. British designer Arne Maynard coordinates the brick-orange flowers of *Fritillaria imperialis* with the juvenile copper-orange foliage of a springtime beech hedge; while Sarah Price in the UK and Ron Lutsko in the

USA both recommend *Cyclamen hederifolium* for planting under an established oak tree.

For plantspeople – head gardeners and nursery folk – nuance of form and colour are key. British gardener and plantsperson Jonny Bruce recommends *Allium obliquum* for its unusually coloured flowerheads, and *New York Times* gardening columnist Margaret Roach notes *Narcissus* 'Thalia' for its distinctive recurved petals and small cups. Seasonality, flowering duration, climate resilience, ephemerality and perenniality all come into play. Some bulbs were chosen in duplicate, or in a few cases triplicate or more. The most nominated bulb was chosen five times, twice by garden designers, and once by a flower grower, a nurseryperson and a garden writer.

As a consequence of environmental change, a gradual shift in our weather patterns is resulting in hotter, drier summers and winters that are wet but less cold, and the focus of gardeners has shifted towards sustainability. What we plant, where and how we plant it, matters and that is reflected in the selections people made and the bulbs that were chosen for inclusion in this book. There is a new emphasis on bulbs that are perennial over single-use hybrids that flower for only one year before needing to be replaced, and so have an inherently higher carbon footprint in their water and fuel usage. A reluctance to throw away spent bulbs, such as tulips, after a single flowering, paired with a more laid-back approach to lawns, has resulted in a trend for multi-coloured combinations of flowers that are the spoils from the garden, naturalized in grass. There is also a renewed awareness that the fertilizers and pesticides used in the production of non-organic bulbs persist in their flowers and leach into soil water, adversely affecting pollinators and soil-dwelling organisms.

With biodiversity in mind, there is a vogue for flowers with simpler, single forms that are lightly distributed on their stems and so less far removed from the flowers found in nature. Species tulips 'as wild as the wolf' (as tulip expert Anna Pavord puts it) are popular, as are more subtle forms of narcissus and gladiolus.

Here, then, are more than 150 flowering bulbs for gardeners, nominated by the world's leading plantspeople and designers, curated and sequenced in four seasonal chapters according to their flowering time, along with practical advice on their planting and cultivation. From the favourite snowdrop of British garden writer and designer Mary Keen and Great Dixter's most regularly used tulip, recommended by head gardener Fergus Garrett, to the allium that spans the seasons, selected by Dutch landscape designer and plantsperson Piet Oudolf, to British garden designer Dan Pearson's favourite lily, each one has proved itself to be special.

What could be more enjoyable than compiling a list of bulbs to grow in your own garden? From the bluest of the blue camassias to a butter-yellow daffodil that leavens brasher cultivars to an ornithogalum that makes everything else shine a little bit brighter, all you need to know is here.

Opposite:
After first flowering in containers, annual tulip bulbs are replanted in rough grass to reflower over subsequent years at Blacklands in Wiltshire, the garden of organic grower Polly Nicholson

Following pages:
Allium cristophii with *Papaver commutatum* 'Ladybird' and *Campanula patula* at Malverleys garden in Hampshire

Late Winter & Early Spring

Galanthus elwesii
 'Mrs Macnamara'

Galanthus nivalis

Galanthus elwesii

Galanthus plicatus
 'E. A. Bowles'

Virescent and green
 snowdrops

Narcissus 'Cedric Morris'

Eranthis hyemalis

Scilla mischtschenkoana
 'Tubergeniana'

Scilla bifolia

Crocus versicolor

Crocus 'Prins Claus'

Crocus tommasinianus

Iris reticulata

Narcissus bulbocodium

Narcissus 'Spoirot'

Narcissus fernandesii
 var. *cordubensis*

Puschkinia scilloides
 var. *libanotica*

Muscari

Erythronium californicum

Erythronium 'Joanna'

Erythronium 'Pagoda'

Narcissus 'Bath's Flame'

Narcissus 'White Lady'

Narcissus 'Falconet'

Narcissus tazetta

Narcissus for naturalizing

Narcissus 'Lucifer'

Narcissus 'Thalia'

Cyclamen repandum

Ipheion

At the start of the year colour is minimal in scale. During the pared-back days of the winter, snowdrops with armoured nibs that are hardened to spear through the frozen ground are the first of the small-flowered bulbs, taking advantage of the window of light in the tree canopy above them or the winter gap in mowing for those growing in grass, to flower and replenish themselves in readiness to bloom again the following year. Along with other small-flowered bulbs, such as winter aconites and muscari, they benefit from being planted in large numbers, mimicking the way they grow in the wild, so that their flowers register together when they open, making pools of early colour.

Many winter-flowering bulbs are particularly suited to growing in pots, requiring minimal water and few other resources, and there is pleasure to be had in mixing and matching small plants with small containers. Growing them in this way also encourages us to appreciate the detail of their flowers. *Iris reticulata* poke up buds in bowls indoors on the windowsill to flower early at the start of the year and then later, outside in clay pots. A collection of small, choice flowering bulbs placed on a doorstep is an uplifting sight, particularly at this time of the year.

Bulbs that flower early or late are also incredibly useful for pollinators. An emergent bumblebee queen in search of her first sip of nectar will find it in the flower of a *Scilla* or crocus. Plant crocus bulbs where their flowers will be in the warmth of the early sun when they open, as they close up on overcast days when fewer pollinators fly. As the daylight lengthens daffodils unfurl in bright and subtle yellows; the opportunistic woodlander *Erythronium* illuminates dappled shade, making it its own; and colour spreads into every corner of the garden.

Galanthus elwesii 'Mrs Macnamara'

Galanthus

Greater snowdrop

Syn. *Galanthus elwesii* 'Milkwood'

Amaryllidaceae

Height
25 cm (10 in)

Position
Partial shade

Growing conditions
Damp soil that doesn't lie wet

Plant in
Late summer ('in the green') or early spring (dormant bulbs)

Flowers in
Early to late winter

Perennial

RHS H5, USDA 4–9

RHS Award of Garden Merit (AGM)

Precocious *Galanthus elwesii* 'Mrs Macnamara' is 'the best of the earlies', notes British garden designer and writer Mary Keen. 'It is often in flower by Christmas and it clumps up well.' A strong grower, it is noticeably taller than most cultivars and has larger flowers. In common with other snowdrops, the leaves have dark, armoured nibs that are hardened to spear through the frozen ground in winter and flower ahead of their competition. Broad, greyish-green foliage marks its spot in the soil from early in winter, followed by slender white flowers that are bold in stature, with long outer petals; each inner petal is marked with a green 'V'. *G. elwesii* 'Mrs Macnamara' will propagate itself underground via offsets to form a single-species sweep of flower.

Standard practice is to plant snowdrops 'in the green' in spring – after flowering and with the last of the foliage in place – to establish and bloom the following year. Alternatively, plant dormant bulbs in late summer, 10 cm (4 in) deep. Once established, leave the foliage in place on the bulb for a minimum of six weeks after flowering, to photosynthesize and replenish resources for the following winter.

Previous pages:
The Ditch at East Lambrook Manor Gardens in Somerset, with hellebores and naturalized snowdrops including *Galanthus nivalis* 'Margery Fish' and *G.* 'Ophelia'

Galanthus nivalis

Galanthus

Common snowdrop

Syn. *Galanthus nivalis* 'Simplex'

Amaryllidaceae

Height
15 cm (6 in)

Position
Partial shade

Growing conditions
Damp soil that doesn't lie wet

Plant in
Late summer (dormant bulb), early spring ('in the green')

Flowers in
Late winter

Perennial

RHS H5, USDA 3–9

RHS Award of Garden Merit (AGM)

Often found in woodlands, on roadsides and under hedge banks, pioneering *Galanthus nivalis* is the wild or common snowdrop, with narrow leaves and simple, single white flowers. It is best planted in number and allowed to make its way opportunistically around the garden. It is often naturalized in grass, where it is fast and early to bloom, taking advantage of the winter gap in mowing to flower and then replenish itself underground, in readiness for its re-emergence the following year. This is one of the most versatile and reliable of the snowdrop tribe, for damp soil that doesn't sit wet, in the shadow of deciduous trees and shrubs.

Dividing clumps of bulbs after flowering is a good way to help it spread. In mid-spring, lift the bulbs with the last of their foliage attached and gently ease them apart into singles. Use the blade of a spade to make slits in the grass, and drop each bulb in, planting to the same depth as they were in the original clump. Push back the turf over and around them and firm it down, leaving the foliage showing above the grass. Snowdrops can also be planted in borders, either planting them 'in the green' in spring – after flowering and with the last of the foliage in place – to establish and bloom the following year. Alternatively, plant dormant bulbs in late summer, 10 cm (4 in) deep. Plant them in moist but well-drained soil that does not dry out in summer – a shady position is ideal.

Galanthus elwesii

Galanthus
Elwes's snowdrop,
giant snowdrop

Amaryllidaceae

Height
20 cm (8 in)

Position
Partial shade

Growing conditions
Damp soil that doesn't lie wet

Plant in
Late summer (dormant bulb),
early spring ('in the green')

Flowers in
Late winter to early spring

Perennial

RHS H5, USDA 3–9

RHS Award of Garden Merit
(AGM)

It is useful to have a snowdrop with a willingness to colonize freely, and for this *Galanthus elwesii* is one of the best. Easy to grow and swift to establish, it multiplies exponentially in its favoured conditions, opening in the window of light before the tree canopy above comes into leaf and benefiting from leaf litter in autumn. Unlike many snowdrops, it is recognizable from a distance, and twice the height of *Galanthus nivalis* (p.25). *G. elwesii* is the most commonly used snowdrop for naturalizing, with chunky, greyish-green foliage and a double green blotch to its inner petals. En masse, it makes distinctive pools of colour, where no single flower dominates. Dormant bulbs, or snowdrops 'in the green' (after flowering, with the last of their foliage attached), dropped into slots made in the soil with a trowel in late summer or late winter, will return reliably every year. The award-winning Somerset-based landscape design studio Urquhart & Hunt recommends threading the bulbs through plantings of crocus and chionodoxa (glory-of-the-snow), which flower soon afterwards and enjoy the same conditions.

   Plant dormant bulbs in late summer, 10 cm (4 in) deep, or 'in the green' in moisture-retentive ground that doesn't lie wet.

Galanthus plicatus
'E. A. Bowles'

Galanthus

Snowdrop

Amaryllidaceae

Height
20 cm (8 in)

Position
Partial shade

Growing conditions
Damp soil that doesn't lie wet

Plant in
Late summer (dormant bulb),
early spring ('in the green')

Flowers in
Late winter to early spring

Perennial

RHS H5, USDA 7–9

RHS Award of Garden Merit
(AGM)

In the quest to find the perfect snowdrop, the best attributes of the genus – robustness, reliability and bright, clear flowers – can be lost, resulting in what gardeners describe as a 'miffy' cultivar: a snowdrop that is temperamental and reluctant to thrive. *Galanthus plicatus* 'E. A. Bowles' is not this. Named for the British horticulturist Edward Augustus Bowles and originally found in his garden in London, it is the easiest snowdrop to grow. It is also the favourite of British nurseryperson and specialist Joe Sharman, known as Mr Snowdrop because of his influence on British and American snowdrop breeding; he describes it as 'vigorous, reliable and easy to grow', adding that 'it should be in every collection'. With broad, bright green leaves and six identical petals (unlike many snowdrops, which have three long and three short tepals), each clear white flower has a rounded and full appearance. It grows well in damp soil in the dappled shade of trees and shrubs, where it will gently extend its reach every year.

Standard practice is to plant snowdrops 'in the green' in spring – after flowering and with the last of their foliage still attached. Alternatively, they can be planted as dormant bulbs in late summer, 10 cm (4 in) deep, when they are full of the stored energy of the previous year.

Virescent and green snowdrops

Position
Partial shade

Growing conditions
Damp soil that doesn't lie wet

Plant in
Late summer (dormant bulb),
early spring ('in the green')

Flowers in
Late winter to early spring

Perennial

RHS H5, USDA 5–9
(USDA 6–9 for *G. gracilis*
and 3–9 for *G.* 'Lady Beatrix
Stanley', 'Ophelia', and
G. nivalis 'Margery Fish')

Galanthus plicatus
'Trymlet'

An easy-to-grow cultivar and
the best 'green' for building
up numbers to make a large
clump quickly. It boasts
distinctive, chunky, cres-
cent-shaped green mark-
ings on the outside of the
petals and a green inverted
'V' shape inside.

Height 20 cm (8 in)

Snowdrops flower early, when gardeners, hungry for signs of life, are happy to rootle on their hands and knees to scrutinize their flowers. To the uninitiated, a snowdrop is just a snowdrop, but for enthusiasts, known as 'galanthophiles', differences in the flower markings and the configuration of the petals or subtle variations in colour make particular snowdrops highly desirable: single bulbs of a rare variety can sell for more than £1,000 ($1,300). Collectible 'green' snowdrops may be marked in green on their inner or outer petals, or have a green wash, known as 'viridescence'; they can be single or double flowered. The double-flowered forms have the additional benefit of opening on overcast days, which single-flowered snowdrops are reluctant to do – making it easier to see their markings. Not all green snowdrops are highly priced; *Galanthus* 'Ophelia', 'Washfield Colesbourne' and 'Magnet' are affordable cultivars and excellent, easy-to-grow plants.

Traditionally snowdrops are planted 'in the green', in spring – after flowering, with the last of their foliage still attached – to establish themselves underground in readiness for flowering the following winter. Experts also plant them as dormant bulbs in late summer, 10 cm (4 in) deep, full of the stored energy of the previous year.

Galanthus gracilis
Slender snowdrop

Graceful flowers with narrow, twisting, grass-like leaves in greyish-green.

Height 12 cm (5 in)

Galanthus 'Lady Beatrix Stanley'

Double flowers with narrow, pointed outer petals and multiple layers of inner petals that are edged in green. An early flowerer, named after the British botanical artist Beatrix Stanley.

Height 12 cm (5 in)

RHS Award of Garden Merit (AGM)

Galanthus 'Magnet'

Syn. *Galanthus nivalis* 'Magnet'

Good green markings on the inner petals. The flowers are held on long, narrow stalks and quiver in the breeze.

Height 16 cm (6 in)

Galanthus nivalis 'Margery Fish'

An easily recognizable snowdrop with distinctive, backward-curving spathes and narrow virescent flowers that are delicate and suited to pot culture. Discovered at East Lambrook, the Somerset garden of writer Margery Fish.

Height 25 cm (10 in)

Galanthus 'Ophelia'

A double-flowered, green-centred variety that is easy to grow and swift to increase.

Height 15 cm (6 in)

Galanthus 'Seagull'

A bigger, robust cultivar with wide, glaucous foliage and broad, honey-scented flowers. Easy to grow.

Height 20 cm (8 in)

Galanthus 'Veronica Cross'

Single flowers with green markings on the outer petals and green inner petals. Flowers in mid-season.

Height 17 cm (7 in)

Galanthus 'Washfield Colesbourne'

Big white flowers with very dark green marks on the inside. Easy to single out and to appreciate the marks.

Height 20 cm (8 in)

Narcissus 'Cedric Morris'

Narcissus

Daffodil

Syn. *Narcissus minor*
'Cedric Morris'

Amaryllidaceae

Height
25 cm (10 in)

Position
Partial shade

Growing conditions
Any soil

Plant in
Autumn

Flowers in
Early to late winter

Perennial

RHS H6, USDA 7a–9

An early-flowering miniature daffodil that is sometimes found blooming on Christmas Day in temperate climates, *Narcissus* 'Cedric Morris' was originally wild-collected (when such practices were legal) in northern Spain by the British artist and plantsperson Cedric Morris (1889–1982). Much sought after as a bulb, it retains the informality of a wildflower with well-proportioned, pale lemon blooms around small, crimped cups. 'A long-flowering variety which will continue to produce cheerful, light yellow trumpets until March,' notes British gardener Jonny Bruce. It is a good companion for other small-flowered treasures, including crocuses (pp.36–8) and *Iris reticulata* (pp.40–41).

Dormant bulbs can be difficult to source, but clumps are easily divided 'in the green' – after flowering and with the last of the foliage still in place – in spring. Otherwise, plant dormant bulbs in autumn, 5 cm (2 in) deep, 10 cm (4 in) apart, in damp soil that is warm in summer, adding a handful of grit under and around each bulb. Bulbs can be slow to increase underground.

Previous pages:
Naturalized snowdrops open their flowers in the window of light before the tree canopy above them comes into leaf at Colesbourne Gardens near Cheltenham in Gloucestershire

Eranthis hyemalis

Eranthis

Winter aconite

Syn. *Aconitum hyemale*

Ranunculaceae

Height
10 cm (4 in)

Position
Full or partial shade

Growing conditions
Any soil

Plant in
Early to mid-autumn

Flowers in
Early spring

Perennial

RHS H6, USDA 3–8

**RHS Award of Garden Merit
(AGM)**

While some bulbs are best grown in small quantities, others are dependent on bigger numbers to make their distinctive pools of colour. The bright yellow, upturned flowers of *Eranthis hyemalis* are held in individual ruffs of green. Margaret Roach, *New York Times* gardening columnist, describes this plant as an early 'trooper', noting that 'it can be slow to establish, but once it begins to self-sow it will make an impressive colony.' Bill Thomas, of Chanticleer Garden in Pennsylvania, recommends growing it from seed, sown fresh in early spring, with a five-year wait from seedling to flower. Easily spotted from on the wing, the flowers are a boon for early pollinators at a time when pollen is scarce.

Plant bulbs 10 cm (4 in) deep with their pointed end up, in autumn, spacing them twice the width of a bulb apart. Then let them meander naturally through grass, borders and the woodland edge.

Scilla mischtschenkoana 'Tubergeniana'

Scilla

Squill

Syn. *Scilla* 'Tubergeniana'

Asparagaceae

Height
10 cm (4 in)

Position
Any aspect

Growing conditions
Damp, well-drained soil

Plant in
Late summer to early autumn

Flowers in
Late winter to early spring

Perennial

RHS H6, USDA 3–8

RHS Award of Garden Merit (AGM)

This is the earliest of the flowering squills, skipping ahead to bloom in late winter alongside snowdrops, crocuses and *Cyclamen coum* as a pretty ingredient in miniature set-piece plantings. Native to the Caucasus region and Iraq, where it grows in the mountains, it has small, pale blue flowers marked with a narrow line of darker blue down the middle of each petal. The stems continue to grow even as the flowers open, with flowers starting to bloom before they are fully clear of the soil and ahead of their foliage, making them easy for early pollinators on the wing to spot. This squill is up to the challenge of growing in a shallow dish or pot alongside other early-flowering treasures; alternatively, it naturalizes easily in the garden, making a beautiful, low detail.

Plant bulbs in the ground 8 cm (3 in) deep in late summer or early autumn, or three to a 20 cm (8 in) pot, in a gritty compost, two parts loam-based to one part horticultural grit, tucking them in alongside other small-flowered bulbs. A topping of grit on the compost will stop the flowers from becoming dirtied in the rain.

Scilla bifolia

Scilla

Alpine squill, two-leaf squill, early spring squill, scilla

Asparagaceae

Height
10 cm (4 in)

Position
Benefits from partial shade after flowering

Growing conditions
Well-drained soil

Plant in
Late autumn

Flowers in
Late winter to early spring

Perennial

RHS H6, USDA 3–8

RHS Award of Garden Merit (AGM)

'Plants sometimes surprise me with unexpected movements, especially in the cold climates where I live,' notes Midori Shintani, head gardener at Tokachi Millennium Forest in northern Japan, a garden that has been designed by British designer Dan Pearson to be sustainable for a thousand years. 'Now, after six years of stubborn silence since planting, *Scilla bifolia* has finally made an appearance.'

In the more temperate conditions of the meadow at Gravetye Manor in Sussex that is the former home and garden of the original 'wild' gardener, William Robinson (1838–1935), this spring bloomer with starry, sky-blue flowers grows among lemon-yellow daffodils and as a prelude to the bluebells. Self-sown seedlings are a good indicator that it has found its favoured spot, with spontaneous generations taking three or four years to reach flowering size.

Plant the small corms 10 cm (4 in) deep and a similar distance apart, adding a handful of grit with each one in heavier soil. The corms' contractile roots enable them to pull themselves deeper if necessary to reach their favoured depth.

Crocus versicolor

Crocus

Crocus

Iridaceae

Height
10 cm (4 in)

Position
Sun

Growing conditions
Any soil

Plant in
Early to mid-autumn

Flowers in
Late winter to early spring

Perennial

RHS H6, USDA 3–8

One of the prettiest in the crocus tribe, this event-of-a-flower is worth seeking out for the resilience of its blooms, which are able to withstand winter wet. Its small lilac petals are striped in deep violet on the reverse and open widely in the warmth of the sun. The foliage is narrow and grass-like, with a slim white stripe along the length of each leaf. Native to the rocky scrub and open woodlands of the Mediterranean, it grows well in stony or grassy places, including under deciduous trees and shrubs. Its season is brief and it is all the more precious for that; the bulbs are dormant by summer. 'Bright and joyful,' notes award-winning Provence-based garden designer James Basson, who is renowned for his expert knowledge of plants that are suited to dry climates, 'especially during the browns of late winter'.

Plant the corms where the flowers will be in the warmth of the sun as they open, 7 cm (3 in) deep, 5 cm (2 in) apart, with their pointed ends up. The corms have contractile roots that enable them to pull themselves deeper if necessary to reach their favoured depth.

Crocus
'Prins Claus'

Crocus

**Crocus 'Prins Claus',
snow crocus**

Syn. *Crocus chrysanthus*
'Prins Claus'

Iridaceae

Height
8 cm (3 in)

Position
Sun

Growing conditions
Any soil

Plant in
Autumn

Flowers in
Late winter to early spring

Perennial

RHS H6, USDA 3–8

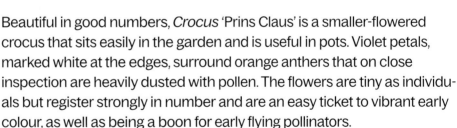

Beautiful in good numbers, *Crocus* 'Prins Claus' is a smaller-flowered crocus that sits easily in the garden and is useful in pots. Violet petals, marked white at the edges, surround orange anthers that on close inspection are heavily dusted with pollen. The flowers are tiny as individuals but register strongly in number and are an easy ticket to vibrant early colour, as well as being a boon for early flying pollinators.

Plant the corms where the winter sun will warm their flowers as they open and stretch widely on sunny days, then shut up when the weather closes in and fewer flying pollinators are about. In autumn, throw a handful in the air and plant them ad hoc, where they land, to imitate their distribution in nature. Plant with their pointed ends up, 15 cm (6 in) deep, making slits in the soil with a trowel and dropping them in before gently firming the soil back. In a pot, use a gritty compost, two parts loam-based to one part horticultural grit, on top of an extra layer of grit 2 cm (¾ in) deep, as sharp drainage is key.

Crocus
tommasinianus

Crocus

Early crocus, snow crocus

Iridaceae

Height
10 cm (4 in)

Position
Sun

Growing conditions
Well-drained soil

Plant in
Autumn

Flowers in
Late winter to early spring

Perennial

RHS H6, USDA 3–8

RHS Award of Garden Merit (AGM)

Early in spring, the Front Meadow at Great Dixter House and Gardens in Northiam, East Sussex, is speckled with *Crocus tommasinianus*, the first in a colourful procession of spring-flowering bulbs: *Narcissus* (daffodils), *Fritillaria meleagris* (snake's head fritillary, p.104) and, later, common and spotted orchids, that are the result of more than a hundred years of self-sowing and dividing. Appearing alongside the snowdrops, the crocus blooms are gone by mid-spring. With a willingness to self-seed in their favoured conditions, the silver-lilac flowers are most deeply coloured inside, and so en masse look paler in bud than when the flowers are fully open. It is also 'the best crocus for under tall, late-emerging perennials', says Cassian Schmidt, former head gardener at the experimental nursery and garden Hermannshof in Weinheim, Germany.

Plant corms in autumn, with their pointed ends up, 15 cm (6 in) deep, into slots made in the grass with a trowel, carefully firming the turf back around them and watering to settle them in the soil.

Iris reticulata

Iris

Dwarf Iris, early bulbous Iris, miniature Iris, reticulated Iris

Iridaceae

Position
Sun

Growing conditions
Good drainage

Plant in
Late summer to early autumn

Flowers in
Late winter

Perennial

RHS H7, USDA 3–8

The English writer and garden designer Vita Sackville-West (1892–1962) carried trays of *I. reticulata* indoors at Sissinghurst Castle Garden, Kent, to enjoy on her desk at close quarters during winter; in northern Europe, pots of flowering miniature irises are sold alongside hippeastrum (pp.196–200), hyacinths (p.82–3) and bunches of forced, cut tulip flowers to brighten the short, dark days of winter. Native to Turkey, the Caucasus mountains and parts of the Middle East, the corms benefit from warm, sunny outdoor conditions. The term *reticulata* refers to the mesh-like coat that surrounds the corms. The species form, *I. reticulata*, has striking deep blue-to-violet petals streaked on their insides with yellow and white, but recent meticulous breeding work has widened the palette of cultivars and the most painterly colours are well worth seeking out.

The corms are best grown in pots, one or two per 10 cm (4 in) container. Use a gritty compost – two parts loam-based to one part horticultural grit – on top of an extra layer of grit, 2 cm (¾ in) deep, as sharp drainage is essential. Plant corms 10 cm (4 in) deep, with the pointed end up, and generously spaced, to avoid overcrowding the flowers. Water once on planting and then more often as the first shoots appear.

Iris reticulata

Striking deep blue-to-violet petals streaked inside with yellow and white.

Height 15 cm (6 in)

Iris 'Blue Note'

Deep purple-blue flowers marked in white and darker at the tips.

Height 15 cm (6 in)

Iris 'Harmony'

One of the earliest to flower, in bi-coloured deep and bright blue flowers marked with yellow-orange and white. A firmly established favourite.

Height 15 cm (6 in)

Iris 'Katharine Hodgkin'

Syn. *Iris histrioides* 'Katharine Hodgkin'

Pale greyish-blue flowers patterned with blue and yellow freckles and stripes.

Height 15 cm (6 in)

RHS Award of Garden Merit (AGM)

Iris 'Scent Sational'

Bright violet flowers marked in orange and white on the petals. Subtly scented.

Height 15 cm (6 in)

Following pages:

Iris reticulata and *Cyclamen coum* make a pretty low-level detail in late winter

Narcissus bulbocodium

Narcissus

Hoop-petticoat daffodil

Syn. *Corbularia bulbocodium*

Amaryllidaceae

Height
15 cm (6 in)

Position
Sun or partial shade

Growing conditions
Well-drained soil

Plant in
Autumn

Flowers in
Late winter

Perennial

RHS H4, USDA 7–9

**RHS Award of Garden Merit
(AGM)**

A small-is-beautiful plantsperson's bulb, this precociously flowering miniature daffodil has a broad, funnel-shaped trumpet and tiny, reflexed petals. Described by American landscape designer Ron Lutsko as 'steadfast and cheerful', it is choice yet straightforward to grow, with a refined form that belies a robust nature. It is best grown in pots as a single-species group, to give the opportunity of closely observing the flowers. It is also a pretty companion for *Muscari latifolium* (grape hyacinth, p.49), which flowers at the same time.

In autumn, add a layer of grit to the base of a shallow container and fill with gritty compost, two parts loam-based to one part horticultural grit. Plant bulbs 8 cm (3 in) deep, three per 15 cm (6 in) pot, and keep outside, watering only once the foliage appears. Bulbs can be forced into flowering a little earlier by standing the pot on a radiator for gentle bottom heat immediately on planting, then moving it into cooler conditions as the first shoots appear.

Narcissus 'Spoirot'

Narcissus

Hoop-petticoat daffodil, white petticoat daffodil

Syn. *Narcissus bulbocodium* 'Spoirot'

Amaryllidaceae

Height
15 cm (6 in)

Position
Sun or partial shade

Growing conditions
Well-drained soil

Plant in
Autumn

Flowers in
Late winter

Perennial

RHS H4, USDA 7–9

RHS Award of Garden Merit (AGM)

A choice cultivar of *Narcissus bulbocodium* (opposite) with pale greenish-white, trumpet flowers, this pretty, small-flowered bulb is useful for studding short grass as part of a tapestry lawn. Because it flowers so early, before the grass has started into its annual growth, the flowers are held clear of the sward despite their minimal height. Planted in this way, *N.* 'Spoirot' makes a good companion to snowdrops as part of a successional planting, with scilla, narcissus and species tulips following on later.

In autumn, use a trowel or hori hori to make slits in the grass and add a small amount of grit. Plant the small bulbs 8 cm (3 in) deep, pointed end up and then carefully push the turf back down. After flowering, wait five or six weeks before mowing the lawn to allow the foliage to photosynthesize and replenish resources in the bulb.

Narcissus fernandesii var. *cordubensis*

Narcissus

Fernandes daffodil

Syn. *Narcissus cordubensis*

Amaryllidaceae

Height
25 cm (10 in)

Position
Sun

Growing conditions
Rich soil

Plant in
Early autumn

Flowers in
Late winter to mid-spring

Perennial

RHS H6, USDA 3–8

A yellow jonquil daffodil, delicate in scale and habit, and early flowering, this is a go-to bulb for discerning gardeners and the favourite of British garden designer and writer Mary Keen. Typically of a jonquil daffodil, the flowers are usually in clusters of three or more, and they are held on a single stem. The flowers register easily above the narrow, grass-like foliage. Bunch-flowering, with a long and well-spaced flowering pattern, it will repeat-flower if cut.

In autumn, plant bulbs 8 cm (3 in) deep, 10 cm (4 in) apart, in damp soil that is on the dry side in summer, adding a handful of grit under and around the bulbs in heavier soil. In common with all daffodils, it is import-ant to leave the spent foliage on the bulb for a minimum of six weeks after flowering, to allow the bulb to replenish itself for the following year.

Puschkinia scilloides var. libanotica

Puschkinia

Lebanon striped squill, striped squill

Syn. *Puschkinia libanotica*

Liliaceae

Height
20 cm (8 in)

Position
Sun or partial shade

Growing conditions
Light soil, damp in spring and dry in summer

Plant in
Early to mid-autumn

Flowers in
Early spring

Perennial

RHS H6, USDA 3–8

RHS Award of Garden Merit (AGM)

Delicate in stature and often overlooked, this exceptionally early and enduring small-flowered squill deserves to be better known. Its light blue flowers are reflexed (bent backwards) the tiniest amount at their tips to form bells, like a miniature hyacinth. It makes a pretty companion to snowdrops that flower at the same time, and is useful for tucking in between the roots of established trees and shrubs, where the soil is mostly taken and moisture is in limited supply, to flower freely ahead of its competition. Reliably perennial, it increases incrementally in number each year.

In autumn, plant the small bulbs 10 cm (4 in) deep and pointed end up, using a trowel or hori hori to work them in and taking care not to damage adjacent roots. Like most squills, it benefits from soil that is damp in spring and on the dry side during the summer.

Muscari

Muscari

Grape hyacinth

Asparagaceae

Position
Sun

Growing conditions
Moist, well-drained soil

Plant in
Autumn

Flowers in
Early to mid-spring

Perennial

RHS H6, USDA 3–8

Muscari are best planted in large numbers to make pools of early colour. The flowers offer a pretty, low-level detail in challenging garden spots and are useful for connecting different parts of the garden. When choosing which cultivars to grow, nuance of colour is key. Matt Collins, head gardener at the Garden Museum in Lambeth, London, recommends *Muscari armeniacum* 'Valerie Finnis' for its 'particular shade of blue, a rare and uniform sky-blue that seems to complement any companion'. *M.* 'Blue Eyes' has ultramarine flowers and 'Ocean Magic' is blue marked in white. The appeal of *M.* 'Golden Fragrance' lies in its gradient colour change, from plum to yellow. British planting designer Noel Kingsbury notes *M. armeniacum* for its papery seedheads after flowering.

Not a rare bulb and valuable for it, muscari colonizes easily and will find its own way in the garden.

In autumn, plant bulbs 10 cm (4 in) deep, 5 cm (2 in) apart. Richer soil will result in more leaf and fewer flowers.

Muscari armeniacum

Armenian grape hyacinth
Mid-blue flowers followed by papery seedheads.

Height 20 cm (8 in)

RHS Award of Garden Merit (AGM)

Muscari armeniacum
'Valerie Finnis'

Syn. *M.* 'Valerie Finnis'

Pale blue flowers and narrow, green foliage. Named for the renowned British gardener and photographer.

Height 20 cm (8 in)

Muscari aucheri
'Ocean Magic'

Blue flowers prettily edged in white.

Height 20 cm (8 in)

Muscari 'Blue Eyes'

Syn. *M. armeniacum* 'Blue Eyes'

Deep violet-blue flowers that are pale at their tips.

Height 20 cm (8 in)

Muscari latifolium

Broad-leaved grape hyacinth

Deep purple-blue flowers with pale blue tips and almost black at the base.

Height 20 cm (8 in)

RHS Award of Garden Merit (AGM)

Muscari neglectum

Syn. *M. grandifolium*

Pale buds open to darkest blue flowers that are rimmed in white.

Height 20 cm (8 in)

Muscari macrocarpum
'Golden Fragrance'

Pretty two-toned flowers and a light scent.

Height 20 cm (8 in)

Following pages:
The flowering of *Muscari armeniacum* is beautifully timed to coincide with the opening of cherry blossom in spring at RHS Wisley garden in Surrey

Erythronium
californicum

Erythronium

Dog's tooth violet, fawn lily

Liliaceae

Height
30 cm (12 in)

Position
Dappled shade

Growing conditions
Cool, damp soil

Plant in
Early autumn to early winter

Flowers in
Early to mid-spring

Perennial

RHS H5, USDA 6–9

A delicate-looking yet opportunistic woodlander that will find its own way in damp soil and dappled shade. It is commonly known as the dog's tooth violet owing to the long, narrow shape of the tuber, and American landscape designer Ron Lutsko describes it as 'graceful, elegant and unsurpassed for poise'. Its pale yellowish-white flowers register easily in low light, held aloft over green foliage that is heavily blotched. The flowers are captivating among deciduous ferns, which will unfurl their croziers as erythronium flowers, making a study in form and texture.

In autumn, plant tubers vertically with the pointed end upwards, 10 cm (4 in) deep and 25 cm (10 in) apart. As with other erythroniums, it doesn't grow well if the tubers have been allowed to dry out ahead of planting, and is often sold as a potted plant. Reliably perennial, it benefits from a mulch of leaf litter in autumn.

Erythronium 'Joanna'

Erythronium

Dog's tooth violet, fawn lily

Liliaceae

Height
25 cm (10 in)

Position
Dappled shade

Growing conditions
Cool, damp soil

Plant in
Early autumn to early winter

Flowers in
Early to mid-spring

Perennial

RHS H4, USDA 6–9

**RHS Award of Garden Merit
(AGM)**

'It is not easy to choose a favourite erythronium,' says plantsperson Jimi Blake of Hunting Brook Gardens in County Wicklow, Ireland, 'but *Erythronium* "Joanna" stands out for its delightfully recurved petals and mutable colour.' Yellow on opening and turning shades of apricot and peach as they age, they are offset by marbled foliage. In common with all erythroniums, it increases readily underground, via offsets, in rich, damp, woodsy soil.

Plant the bulbs in autumn, with the pointed end upwards, 10–15 cm (4–6 in) deep in dappled shade. Keep the soil damp until the bulbs have established. A mulch of leaf litter in autumn will benefit the following spring's flowers. It is easy to propagate by lifting and dividing clumps after flowering. It is often sold as a potted plant in late spring and early summer.

Erythronium
'Pagoda'

Erythronium

Dog's tooth violet, fawn lily

Liliaceae

Height
30 cm (12 in)

Position
Dappled shade

Growing conditions
Cool, damp soil

Plant in
Early autumn to early winter

Flowers in
Early to mid-spring

Perennial

RHS H5, USDA 6–9

RHS Award of Garden Merit
(AGM)

This easy-going woodlander for cool, damp shade is willing to naturalize under deciduous trees and shrubs. Its nodding, swept-back flowers are held on short, narrow stems above mottled green leaves. It is a good companion for cowslips (*Primula veris*) and oxlips (*Primula elatior*) in a combination that is reminiscent of an English woodland floor in spring-time, both plants taking advantage of the winter window of light before the tree canopy above comes into leaf. *Erythronium* 'Pagoda' is a small vignette of a flower in sulphur yellow, marked in the middle with a smudge of brown. Expect around ten nodding flowers from a tuber.

In autumn, plant tubers as soon as you receive them, since they are prone to drying out. Plant 10 cm (4 in) deep in cool, humus-rich soil. Alternatively, it is often sold as a potted plant in late spring and summer.

Opposite:

Early-flowering *Erythronium* 'Pagoda' is happy in cool, damp soil in partial shade, planted here beneath the cherry tree *Prunus* 'Matsumae-kofuku' at RHS Wisley garden in Surrey

Narcissus 'Bath's Flame'

Narcissus

Daffodil

Amaryllidaceae

Height
50 cm (20 in)

Position
Sun or partial shade

Growing conditions
Any soil

Plant in
Early autumn

Flowers in
Early spring

Perennial

RHS H6, USDA 3–8

A pale lemon daffodil, with a pretty twist to its outer petals and a small, straw-yellow cup with an orange lip. The flowers, which are produced one flower to a stem, hold their colour well. *N.* 'Bath's Flame' is part of the 'small-cupped' group of daffodils – those with trumpets that measure less than one-third of the length of their petals. Over recent years there has been a trend for more delicate forms of narcissus that sit easily in semi-wild plantings, and 'Bath's Flame' is at once just wild and just cultivated enough.

In autumn, plant bulbs 15 cm (6 in) deep, in groups of eight to ten, in soil that is damp in spring and warm and on the dry side in summer. This daffodil is truly perennial: it will increase in number underground, making bigger clumps each year. After flowering, remove the spent blooms to divert energy into building up the reserves in the bulb rather than making seed, and leave the fading foliage on the bulb to allow photosynthesis to take place to replenish food stores inside, ready for flowering the following year.

Narcissus
'White Lady'

Narcissus

Daffodil

Amaryllidaceae

Height
40 cm (16 in)

Position
Sun or partial shade

Growing conditions
Any soil

Plant in
Early autumn

Flowers in
Early to mid-spring

Perennial

RHS H6, USDA 3–8

A firmly established favourite, valued for its white flowers with a slight twist to their petals surrounding a pale lemon cup. At Hunting Brook Gardens in County Wicklow, Ireland, plantsperson Jimi Blake grows it as part of a colourful, textural combination, threaded among *Narcissus* 'Segovia' and *N.* 'Polar Ice', with early-flowering perennials such as *Geum* 'Scarlet Tempest' and *G.* 'Totally Tangerine' (avens), and dark-stemmed *Pseudopanax crassifolius* (the lancewood tree). A heritage cultivar bred for the cut-flower trade in the 1890s, the flowers are delicate in scale and full of scent. British gardening writer Kendra Wilson describes it as 'a discreet old variety...prim and pale, but still very much a daffodil'.

Plant bulbs in early autumn, 20 cm (8 in) deep, in gritty soil with their pointed ends up. After flowering, remove the spent blooms to divert energy into building up the reserves in the bulb rather than making seed, and leave the foliage on the bulb for a minimum of six weeks to photosynthesize and replenish bulbs for the following year.

Narcissus 'Falconet'

Narcissus

Daffodil

Amaryllidaceae

Height
45 cm (18 in)

Position
Sun or partial shade

Growing conditions
Any soil

Plant in
Early autumn

Flowers in
Early spring

Perennial

RHS H6, USDA 3-8

RHS Award of Garden Merit
(AGM)

A wonderfully scented, bunch-flowering narcissus with small, bright yellow flowers, each with a small orange cup, this is a favourite of British planting designer Noel Kingsbury. Originally bred in Cornwall for the British cut-flower market, it is perfect for the role: easy to grow, very perennial and super-long-flowering, including when cut. Cut the flower stems when the buds are plump to watch them unfurl over the course of a week. There is nothing better for a large jug on the kitchen table.

Like all daffodils, the bulbs benefit from a long time underground, as they will start to grow roots immediately after planting. Plant 20 cm (8 in) deep, 8 cm (3 in) apart and with the pointed end up. Leave the foliage in place on the bulbs for a minimum of six weeks after flowering to photosynthesize and replenish the bulb's resources to flower the following spring. Removing spent blooms will also divert energy into building up the reserves in the bulb rather than making seed.

Narcissus tazetta

Narcissus

Bunch-flowered daffodil

Syn. *N. etruscus*

Amaryllidaceae

Height
50 cm (20 in)

Position
Sun

Growing conditions
Good drainage

Plant in
Early autumn

Flowers in
Early to mid-spring

Perennial

RHS H4, USDA 3–8

The only British outdoor-grown cut flower that is available to buy in the UK in winter, for more than 150 years *Narcissus tazetta* has been cultivated on the flower farms of Cornwall and the Isles of Scilly, to supply London's markets. Bunch-flowering with up to ten flowers per tall stem, the pretty, small flowers are hypnotically scented, with a subtle twist to their foliage. Just a few are enough to fill a vase – and a room with fragrance. It is commonly spotted growing wild in the Mediterranean and, despite having been heavily cultivated, retains the poise of a wildflower. 'In its natural form it cannot get big enough or bright enough ever to be too much,' says Provence-based garden designer James Basson.

Plant bulbs 8 cm (3 in) deep, in soil that is damp in spring. They benefit from a warm summer bake, which initiates the formation of flower buds inside the bulb for the following year.

Narcissus for naturalizing

Narcissus

Daffodil

Amaryllidaceae

Position
Sun or partial shade

Growing conditions
Fertile soil

Plant in
Early autumn

Flowers in
Early to late spring

Perennial

RHS H6, USDA 3–8

Naturalizing is the process of planting bulbs and then leaving them in place after flowering to propagate themselves underground and multiply, emulating the patterns they make in nature. It works best using bulbs that are perennial and have flowers with simpler forms that sit easily in nature. Other things to look out for are narrow foliage that is easily lost among grass after flowering and self-seeding tendencies, which will help increase its numbers further. Troy Scott Smith, head gardener at Sissinghurst Castle in Kent, describes the wild daffodil *Narcissus pseudonarcissus* as his 'go-to choice, flowering in March to last for a number of weeks.'

To naturalize daffodils, plant bulbs in autumn, using the blade of a spade to make slits in the soil or grass, and plant each bulb 15 cm (6 in) deep, with its pointed end up. Push back the soil or turf around the bulb and firm it down, watering to settle it in, especially if the soil is dry. After flowering, leave the foliage in place for at least six weeks to photosynthesize and build up resources in the bulbs for the following year. Remove the seedheads only once they have opened and dispersed their seed, which happens in late spring and early summer.

Narcissus 'Jack Snipe'

Syn. *N. cyclamineus* 'Jack Snipe'

A pretty miniature daffodil with one flower per stem. White petals surround a bright yellow trumpet. Mid-spring flowering.

Height 20 cm (8 in)

RHS Award of Garden Merit (AGM)

Narcissus 'Hawera'

Syn. *N. triandrus* 'Hawera'

A miniature, bunch-flowering variety with lemon-yellow flowers.

Height 20 cm (8 in)

RHS Award of Garden Merit (AGM)

Narcissus obvallaris

Tenby daffodil

Syn. *N. pseudonarcissus* subsp. *obvallaris*

A British native, found in Tenby, Wales, with bright yellow flowers and trumpets.

Height 30 cm (12 in)

Narcissus poeticus 'Recurvus'

Old pheasant's eye daffodil

Reflexed flowers with yellow trumpets, marked in red at their tips. Scented and late to flower.

Height 40 cm (16 in)

RHS Award of Garden Merit (AGM)

Narcissus pseudonarcissus

Wild daffodil, Lent lily daffodil

A British native with lemon petals and a darker yellow trumpet; it is good for self-seeding.

Height 35 cm (14 in)

Following pages:

Naturalized planting of *Narcissus poeticus* 'Recurvus' with *Fritillaria meleagris* in long grass at Hanham Court Gardens, near Bristol

Narcissus 'Lucifer'

Narcissus

Daffodil

Amaryllidaceae

Height
40 cm (16 in)

Position
Sun or partial shade

Growing conditions
Any soil

Plant in
Early autumn

Flowers in
Early spring

Perennial

RHS H6, USDA 3–8

Pairing simplicity of form with the robustness of a modern hybrid, *Narcissus* 'Lucifer' is a beguiling flower. Soft lemon petals deepen in colour towards the middle of the flower, surrounding a zesty orange trumpet. The petals have a dissolved feel to their edges, giving the flower a light, diaphanous air that sits easily as part of a semi-wild planting. Sturdy and rob, it clumps up well. Plant it in single-species groups, to push up between the light-limbed emergent foliage of later-flowering perennials.

Bulbs are best planted in early autumn, since they will immediately begin to put down roots on planting. Plant them 15 cm (6 in) deep in soil that is damp in spring and on the dry side in summer. After flowering, remove the spent blooms to divert energy into building up the reserves in the bulb rather than making seed, and leave the foliage in place for a minimum of six weeks to photosynthesize and replenish resources in the bulb for the following spring.

Narcissus 'Thalia'

Narcissus

Daffodil, triandus daffodil

Amaryllidaceae

Height
45 cm (18 in)

Position
Sun or partial shade

Growing conditions
Any soil

Plant in
Early autumn

Flowers in
Early to mid-spring

Perennial

RHS H6, USDA 3–8

A nodding, bunch-flowering daffodil with flowers that start soft yellow, moving to milk-white as they age, *Narcissus* 'Thalia' is lovely studded among more brashly yellow daffodils to add depth and leaven their colour. The flowers are distinctly recurved, with small cups. It is a favourite with garden designers and landscape architect Miguel Urquijo recommends it for its reliability and resilience, saying 'it is easy to combine with other plants and does well in both sun and shade, even tolerating the demanding conditions under umbrella pines (*Pinus pinea*) and holm oaks (*Quercus ilex*). After flowering, its leaves remain tidy extending its post flowering presence for at least another three weeks. It also has a lovely elegant scent.'

Plant bulbs 15 cm (6 in) deep with their pointed end up in early autumn. The bulb starts putting down roots straight away and benefits from a longer time in the soil. It will flower into late spring. After flower-ing, remove the spent blooms to divert energy into building up the reserves in the bulb rather than making seed, and leave the foliage in place on the bulb for a minimum of six weeks to photosynthesize and replenish its resources for the following spring.

Cyclamen
repandum

Cyclamen

Wavy-edged cyclamen

Primulaceae

Height
15 cm (6 in)

Position
Partial shade

Growing conditions
Any soil

Plant in
Mid-autumn or
mid-spring

Flowers in
Early to mid-spring

Perennial

RHS H4, USDA 7b–10

**RHS Award of Garden
Merit (AGM)**

A favourite of British garden designer Sarah Price, this elfin cyclamen has an arrestingly beautiful form and is notable for its narrowly pointed, slightly wavy petals. In common with other members of the cyclamen family, its flowers tilt strongly downwards. Price is recognized for favouring plants that remain close to their wild parents, and *Cyclamen repandum* fits this brief comfortably. It is a pretty companion for primroses (*Primula vulgaris*) and the emergent lacy croziers of deciduous ferns, tucked into rooty places, underneath deciduous trees and shrubs, where it benefits from the leaf litter.

In autumn, plant tubers 5 cm (2 in) deep and irregularly spaced. Alternatively, buy it as a young plant in a pot in spring, which has the additional advantage of allowing you to choose one with silver-speckled foliage. In leaf throughout winter, it is dormant by summer.

Ipheion

Ipheion

Spring starflower

Amaryllidaceae

Height
15 cm (6 in)

Position
Full sun

Growing conditions
Well-drained soil

Plant in
Autumn

Flowers in
Late winter to late spring and
early autumn

Perennial

RHS H5, USDA 5–9

Right:
Ipheion uniflorum
'Wisley Blue'

Lilac-blue flowers marked
in lilac.

**RHS Award of Garden Merit
(AGM)**

Opposite:
Ipheion 'Alberto Castillo'

Narrow, greyish-blue leaves
and white star flowers with
a faint dark stripe. Easy in a
sheltered spot.

**RHS Award of Garden
Merit (AGM)**

Native to South Africa and commonly known as the starflower
or spring starflower, *Ipheion* are tenacious, adaptable and easy-
to-keep small-flowered bulbs, best grown where the sun can
open their flowers. *I.* 'Alberto Castillo' is one of the prettiest. Held
on short, dark stems, each star-shaped flower has a yellow eye
and a narrow stripe down the middle of each of its petals. At the
Garden Museum in Lambeth, London, it grows in the café border
in a patch of soil, in the lee of the River Thames, with *Epimedium*
'Sulphurium' and *Iris lazica*. Long-flowering, it will repeat-flower
in autumn in its favoured conditions. *I. uniflorum* 'Wisley Blue' is
a good alternative for a more colourful combination.

Plant bulbs in autumn, 8 cm (3 in) deep, 10 cm (4 in) apart
with their pointed ends up. It is easy to propagate by lifting the
bulbs after they have finished flowering and carefully detaching
a few, which can be replanted immediately.

Late Spring

Trillium kurabayashii

Anemone nemorosa
 'Robinsoniana'

Anemone blanda

Leucojum aestivum

Leucojum aestivum
 'Gravetye Giant'

Outdoor hyacinths

Species tulips

Tulipa 'Lady Jane'

Tulipa 'Sarah Raven'

Tulipa 'Violet Beauty'

Perennial tulips

Tulipa 'Black Parrot'

English Florists' tulips

Modern Rembrandt tulips

Fritillaria meleagris

Fritillaria uva-vulpis

Fritillaria acmopetala

Fritillaria michailovskyi

Fritillaria imperialis

Fritillaria persica

Ornithogalum umbellatum

Tropaeolum tricolor

Allium siculum

Allium tripedale

Asphodelus albus

Benton irises

Dichelostemma capitatum

Scilla peruviana

Spring happens before you can see it, deep down underground where, stirred by lengthening days and rising temperatures, bulbs are preparing to be pulled up to the light, an annual fixture in the gardening year for fast and easy colour.

The flowering of *Leucojum* (Lodden lily) is perfectly timed to coordinate with the opening of spring blossom, and in partial shade *Ipheion* 'Alberto Castillo' reveals the first of a succession of flowers. A procession of tulips, led by the species varieties – *Tulipa humilis*, followed by *T. turkestanica* and *T. clusiana* – and later the rich and dark, and brilliant and bright annual and perennial forms, comes into flower. Dark velvet-hued *T.* 'Black Parrot' is, as British gardener Arthur Parkinson puts it, the tulip for pots 'like huge, living vases of flowers'.

There is a current vogue for flowers with simpler, single forms, akin to those found in nature. *Allium tripedale* hits this brief, its asymmetrical flowers sitting comfortably in wilder-style gardens that are designed to be in step with nature. Dainty *Fritillaria acmopetala* occupies the niche for a pretty, easy-to-grow bulb with a flower in a fashionably off-beat colour.

Perennial bulbs are generally the best choice for ecological reasons, and those that have a permanent home outside also lend themselves to uninhibited picking. The blooms of many spring-flowering bulbs last a long time as cut flowers, and some, such as tulips, continue to grow once picked.

The late spring is marked with a surge of growth and a sharpening of the senses. These flowering bulbs earn their keep before the year tilts into summer.

Trillium
kurabayashii

Trillium

Giant purple wake robin

Melanthiaceae

Height
60 cm (24 in)

Position
Shade or partial shade

Growing conditions
Humus-rich soil

Plant in
Early to late autumn

Flowers in
Early to mid-spring

Perennial

RHS H4, USDA 7b–9

A woodlander and North American wildflower that meanders to form textural colonies in deep and dappled shade. As soon as temperatures rise in spring, its green leaves, with dark and silver markings, push up through the ground, followed by deep red flowers, each with three petals, that sit immediately upon them. At Tokachi Millennium Forest in Hokkaido, Japan, *Trillium kurabayashii* grows with candelabra primula (*Primula* sp.) on the floor of an oak woodland, both plants benefiting from the window of light before the tree canopy above them comes into leaf, and from the leaf litter in autumn.

Plant the woody rhizomes just below the surface of damp, woodsy soil in early autumn, watering after planting, especially if the weather is dry. The rhizomes are sold freshly lifted, often in bags of damp sawdust or compost, and should be planted immediately; they do not grow well if they have been allowed to dry out.

Anemone nemorosa 'Robinsoniana'

Anemone

Wood anemone

Ranunculaceae

Height
15 cm (6 in)

Position
Partial shade

Growing conditions
Damp, well-drained soil

Plant in
Early to mid-autumn

Flowers in
Early to mid-spring

Perennial

RHS H5, USDA 3–8

RHS Award of Garden Merit (AGM)

Anemone nemorosa 'Robinsoniana' is an early flowerer for partial shade in slightly damp, woodsy soil. It has delicately divided leaves and pale blue flowers that have a luminous quality in low light, creating a hypnotic effect en masse. In the wild, it is an indicator species for ancient woodland. Plant the rhizomes where the flowers will be in the sun when they open, as they open more widely on sunny days, offering early forage for pollinators on the wing.

The rhizomes are twig-like and most easily started in pots of loam-based compost, to be transplanted into the garden when their first shoots appear. Soak them in tepid water overnight before planting – they will double in size – then plant horizontally, 2 cm (just under 1 in) below the surface of the compost. When the first shoots have pushed up, move them outside, planting to the same depth as they were in their pots.

Anemone blanda

Anemone

Windflower

Ranunculaceae

Height
15 cm (6 in)

Position
Sun or dappled shade

Growing conditions
Any soil

Plant in
Mid-autumn

Flowers in
Early to mid-spring

Perennial

RHS H6, USDA 3–8

RHS Award of Garden Merit (AGM)

A member of the buttercup family that demonstrates its strength by spreading swiftly, making it a great choice for naturalized plantings. Myriad blue daisy-like flowers with acid-yellow middles straighten their stems and open wide in the warmth of the early sun, offset by prettily cut, dark green foliage. Commonly, it is known as the windflower, as the flowers turn their faces away from the wind and close up on overcast days. Native to the Mediterranean, where it grows in gravel or scree, it makes a beautiful low detail, including as a prelude to species tulips that flower soon afterwards.

Soak the twig-like rhizomes in tepid water overnight before planting to encourage their shoots; they will double in size. Outside, plant horizontally, 7 cm (3 in) deep, 10 cm (4 in) apart. The corms have the ability to adjust their depth by means of contractile roots, so they will pull themselves deeper if necessary to reach their ideal depth. An adaptable and easy bulb.

Leucojum aestivum

Leucojum

Lodden lily, summer snowflake

Amaryllidaceae

Height
30 cm (12 in)

Position
Sun or dappled shade

Growing conditions
Damp ground

Plant in
Autumn

Flowers in
Early to mid-spring

Perennial

RHS H7, USDA 3–8

Not a snowdrop but often taken for one, *Leucojum aestivum* is taller and later flowering, with six uniform petals, dotted green at the tips. Each stout little flower is held 30 cm (12 in) high. 'It wakes up early and by March is already exerting a presence in the garden' (see opposite), says Troy Scott Smith, head gardener at Sissinghurst Castle Garden in Kent. Best suited to damp conditions, it is a good companion for snake's head fritillary (*Fritillaria meleagris*, p.104), including in grass as part of a damp meadow. Slightly shorter than its offspring, *L. aestivum* 'Gravetye Giant' (p.80), it is still tall enough for its flower to be seen easily above longer grass. Robust and reliable, it clumps up well.

In autumn, plant bulbs 15 cm (6 in) deep in damp soil, with their pointed ends up. Water once on planting, particularly if the weather is dry, and leave the foliage in place after flowering for a few weeks to replenish the bulbs' resources.

Opposite:
Spring-flowering *Leucojum aestivum* along the Lime Walk at Sissinghurst Castle Garden in Kent

Leucojum aestivum 'Gravetye Giant'

Leucojum

Lodden lily, summer snowflake

Syn. *Leucojum aestivum* 'Gravetye'

Amaryllidaceae

Height
40 cm (16 in)

Position
Partial shade

Growing conditions
Damp soil

Plant in
Early to late autumn

Flowers in
Early to late spring

Perennial

RHS H7, USDA 3–8

RHS Award of Garden Merit (AGM)

Tom Coward is the head gardener behind the progressive, colour-filled flower garden at Gravetye Manor in Sussex, the former home and garden of the visionary nineteenth-century naturalist and wild gardener William Robinson. In 1924 Robinson selected *Leucojum aestivum* 'Gravetye Giant' as a tall form of *L. aestivum* (p.78) after seeing it growing in the garden, and Coward continues to use it as part of the planting there today. He describes it as 'a particularly good form that is robust and long flowering'. Thriving in damp soil, at Gravetye it is naturalized in grass that is sodden all winter, on the periphery of a meadow and under a canopy of deciduous trees – its flowering coincides with the opening of the blossom. It is one of the best bulbs for a late spring meadow.

Plant in small clusters, 15 cm (6 in) deep, in soil that doesn't dry out completely during summer. After flowering, leave the foliage in place on the bulb to replenish its resources for the following year.

Outdoor hyacinths

Hyacinthus

Common hyacinth

Asparagaceae

Height
30 cm (12 in)

Position
Sun, partial shade

Growing conditions
Well-drained soil

Plant in
Early to late autumn

Flowers in
Early to mid-spring

Perennial

RHS H4, USDA 3–8

Right:

H. orientalis 'Anastasia'

Syn. *H.* 'Multiflora Anastacia'
Star-shaped pale blue flowers
with a delicious scent.

Opposite:

H. orientalis 'Woodstock'

Rich, beetroot-coloured
flowers. The best of the
dark-flowered hyacinths.

Hyacinths can be tricky to place in the garden, as their dense, jam-packed flowers register heavily and so feel far removed from the typically small flower forms of early spring. A good way to counter their heft is to replicate the sparsity of their distribution patterns in nature and limit the palette of colours used. The blue florets of *Hyacinthus orientalis* 'Anastasia' are widely distributed on the stems and reminiscent of English bluebells (*Hyacinthoides non-scripta*), making it a good counterpart to more densely packed varieties. The blue hyacinths also tend to be more heavily scented. *H.* 'Woodstock' is the darkest of the deeply coloured cultivars, with intense beetroot-plum flowers. Plant the two at irregular spacing, including the occasional outlier, choosing a spot where the sun will warm their flowers when they open to maximize their fragrance.

In autumn, plant bulbs 10 cm (4 in) deep in sharply drained soil, adding a handful of grit or sand under and around each bulb.

Species tulips

Tulipa
Liliaceae

Plant in
Late autumn to early winter

Flowers in
Early to late spring

Perennial

RHS H6, USDA 3–8
(USDA 5–8 for *T. sprengeri*)

Garden designers have become increasingly smitten with species tulips in recent years. In 2006, brilliant red *T. sprengeri* made the front page of *The Times*, when designer Cleve West used it in his RHS Chelsea flower show garden. Long-lived and more subtle than hybrid tulips, the species are unmatched for beauty and simplicity. Relatively easy to grow, including from seed, in favoured conditions they increase in number underground to make bigger clumps each year.

Swedish designer Ulf Nordfjell recommends scattering bronze-red *T. orphanidea* (Whittallii Group) among the emergent foliage of early-flowering perennials such as salvias and irises, to provide contrast. In the Delos Garden at Sissinghurst Castle Garden in Kent, designer Dan Pearson selected the wild tulip, *T. saxatilis*, to thread between false dittany (*Pseudodictamnus mediterraneus*), yarrow (*Achillea coarctata*) and tussock grasses.

Plant bulbs 10 cm (4 in) deep, 5 cm (2 in) apart, adding a handful of grit. Benefiting from a cold snap, they can be planted in midwinter. Post-flower, leave the foliage in place for at least six weeks, to replenish bulbs for the following year. Remove seedheads in summer, when they have opened and dispersed their seeds.

Tulipa sprengeri

Sprenger tulip

A late flowerer, with 'small pillar-box red flowers carried on narrow stems', according to Fergus Garrett, head gardener at Great Dixter in Sussex. He adds, 'The flowers are followed by decorative seedheads. Unusual in its preference for damp conditions in dappled shade.'

Height 30 cm (12 in); partial shade, damp soil that doesn't lie wet

RHS Award of Garden Merit (AGM)

Tulipa clusiana

Clusius's tulip, lady tulip

Soft pink, yellow-edged flowers that are as good in bud as in flower.

Height 30 cm (12 in); sun, well-drained soil

Tulipa humilis

Low-growing tulip

A short tulip with foliage held almost flat to the ground. The flowers vary in colour, from pale to dark pink; tepals may be tinged from grey-green to blue-black.

Height 25 cm (10 in); sun, well-drained soil

Tulipa orphanidea (Whittallii Group)

Tulip Whittallii Group

Brick-orange flowers with dark middles. Easy to grow and vigorous.

Height 30 cm (12 in); sun, well-drained soil

RHS Award of Garden Merit (AGM)

Tulipa saxatilis

Candia tulip, Cretan rock tulip

Pale pink flowers with a subtle scent open to reveal a distinct yellow blotch to the base of the petals.

Height 15 cm (6 in); sun, well-drained soil

Tulipa sylvestris

Wild tulip

Matt Collins at London's Garden Museum recommends this 'with its gently curved, slender stems and bold yellow flowers'. Grows well in dappled shade.

Height 25 cm (10 in); partial shade, damp soil

Tulipa turkestanica

Turkestan tulip

An excellent choice for pots, naturalizing or to use in a wild garden. Star-shaped, white flowers that are deep yellow-orange at the base.

Height 30 cm (12 in); sun, well-drained soil

Following pages:
Tulipa orphanidea (Whittallii Group) naturalized in grass with primroses and other spring-flowering bulbs at Allt-y-Bela garden in Monmouthshire, Wales

Tulipa 'Lady Jane'

Tulipa

Tulip

Syn. *Tulipa clusiana*
'Lady Jane'

Liliaceae

Height
25 cm (10 in)

Position
Sun

Growing conditions
Well-drained soil

Plant in
Early autumn to
midwinter

Flowers in
Mid-spring

Perennial

RHS H6, USDA 3–8

**RHS Award of Garden
Merit (AGM)**

Dutch designer and plantsperson Piet Oudolf's tulip of choice, *Tulipa* 'Lady Jane', was used in his plantings for the High Line in New York and the Vitra Campus Garden in Weil am Rhein, Germany, where its small, bright, narrow flowers push up among the emergent foliage of summer-flowering plants. The flower has an immediate appeal and is reminiscent of a wild tulip: rosy red on the outer petals and white inside with round, brown papery seedheads later on. 'Colour is only there for a month or two,' Oudolf says. 'The plants that I choose in my designs often have another life after flowering.'

The bulbs are small and can be planted as late as midwinter, as they benefit from a cold snap afterwards. Plant 10 cm (4 in) deep in gritty soil, adding an extra handful of grit underneath. After flowering, leave the foliage on the bulb for a minimum of six weeks so that it can photosynthesize and replenish its reserves for the following year.

Tulipa
'Sarah Raven'

Tulipa

Tulip

Liliaceae

Height
60 cm (24 in)

Position
Sun

Growing conditions
Well-drained soil

Plant in
Late autumn

Flowers in
Mid- to late spring

Annual

RHS H6, USDA 3–8

Few people have had a greater influence on the choice of bulbs that British gardeners grow than the broadcaster and gardener Sarah Raven. For more than 30 years she has trialled a vast number of bulbs and other plants at Perch Hill, her private garden in Sussex, to recommend her favourites for colourful combinations. It stands to reason that the tulip named after her is one of the best. 'During a visit to a tulip trial field in Holland several years ago, I spotted it several rows off,' she notes. 'It has a typical, elegant, pointy-petalled, lily-flowered shape and is true crimson-black. Unlike others, this tulip keeps its richness of colour even as the flowers develop.'

Plant bulbs in groups of eight to ten, 15 cm (6 cm) deep in late autumn, adding a handful of grit around them in heavier soils to ensure they do not sit wet.

Tulipa
'Violet Beauty'

Tulipa

Tulip

Liliaceae

Height
60 cm (24 in)

Position
Sun

Growing conditions
Well-drained soil

Plant in
Late autumn

Flowers in
Mid-to late spring

Annual

RHS H6, USDA 3–8

A pretty and mutable tulip, with violet flowers that lighten as they age, *Tulipa* 'Violet Beauty' lends itself to repeated plantings in a single-species group. In common with other single late tulips, it is tall with sturdy stems and flowers that stand up well to inclement weather. Its flower has a simplicity of form that is ideal for naturalistic planting. In the Little North Garden at Sissinghurst in Kent, it flowers among the emergent foliage of biennials and later-flowering perennials, including melic grass (*Melica altissima* 'Alba'), cow parsley (*Anthriscus sylvestris*) and the fat, felty leaves of yellow mullein (*Verbascum bombyciferum*). Planted in groups at random spacing, it feels spontaneous, as if it has found its own way into the garden.

Plant bulbs in groups of eight to ten, at irregular spacing, 15 cm (6 in) deep in late autumn. Add a handful of grit around each bulb in heavier soils to ensure they don't sit wet.

Following pages:
Tulips, including *Tulipa* 'Violet Beauty', 'Bleu Aimable' and 'Queen of Night' in the Purple Border in the Top Courtyard at Sissinghurst Castle Garden in Kent

Perennial tulips

Tulipa

Tulip

Liliaceae

Position
Sun

Growing conditions
Well-drained soil

Plant in
Late autumn

Flowers in
Mid- to late spring

Perennial

RHS H6, USDA 3–8

As we have seen with fast fashion and single-use plastic, the disposable nature of tulip bulbs has a significant carbon footprint, owing both to the water used to produce the bulbs commercially and to the fuel required for their transport. A more sustainable approach is to choose varieties that are reliably perennial and plant them once, to flower again year after year. Perennial tulips are mainly the Viridiflora types, which have a green mark to the middle of their petals, early-flowering Fosteriana types, parrot and lily-flowered tulips.

While most tulip bulbs flower only once, using up all their resources to do so, these tulips produce new, small bulbs, called offsets, next to the original bulb, and these are big enough to flower. One indicator that this is happening is the appearance of non-flowering shoots right next to the original bulb when it flowers. Left in the soil, these tulips will grow into beautifully wild-looking clumps with flowers of different sizes and heights.

In late autumn, plant bulbs 15 cm (6 in) deep with their pointed ends up, adding a handful of grit with each bulb.

Tulipa 'Black Hero'

A tall, double form
with near-black flowers.

Height 60 cm (24 in)

Tulipa 'Angélique'

A late-flowering, mutable, double form that deepens in colour as it ages.

Height 45 cm (18 in)

RHS Award of Garden Merit (AGM)

Tulipa 'Artist'

A Viridiflora type. Muted orange flowers with a green flash to the petals.

Height 30 cm (12 in)

Tulipa 'Ballerina'

A lily-flowered tulip in bright, sherbet orange. The most regularly grown tulip at Great Dixter in Sussex, where it lines the path from the High Garden to the Peacock Garden.

Height 60 cm (24 in)

RHS Award of Garden Merit (AGM)

Tulipa 'Orange Princess'

A double late form with layers of rich orange petals.

Height 30 cm (12 in)

RHS Award of Garden Merit (AGM)

Tulipa 'Spring Green'

A Viridiflora type, with fresh green-and-white petals. 'A reliable and beautiful tulip that feels at home almost anywhere,' notes Troy Scott Smith of Sissinghurst, Kent.

Height 45 cm (18 in)

RHS Award of Garden Merit (AGM)

Tulipa 'Virichic'

A Viridiflora type. Rich pink flowers with a green flash to the petals.

Height 45 cm (18 in)

Following pages:
Perennial tulip planting with *Tulipa* 'Virichic', 'Black Hero' and 'Request' at Blacklands garden in Wiltshire, the home of organic grower Polly Nicholson

Tulipa
'Black Parrot'

Tulipa

Parrot tulip

Liliaceae

Height
45 cm (18 in)

Position
Sun

Growing conditions
Well-drained soil

Plant in
Late autumn

Flowers in
Mid- to late spring

Annual

RHS H6, USDA 3–8

'If I had to plant just one tulip, it would be this one,' notes British gardener and writer Arthur Parkinson. 'It is the best of the velvets.' He grows it in pots – 'like huge, living vases of flowers' – with the orange, lily-flowered *Tulipa* 'Ballerina' (p.95) and *T.* 'Prinses Irene' (p.103). *T.* 'Black Parrot' is near-black with a hint of plum, the edges of its petals deeply fringed.

Plant bulbs 20 cm (8 in) deep, 8 cm (3 in) apart, in large pots with a gritty mix, two parts compost to one part horticultural grit. Water the bulbs once on planting to settle them in and encourage their roots, and then regularly as the foliage and flowers appear. Parkinson recommends using sprigs of holly on the surface of the compost to protect the newly planted bulbs from being taken by squirrels.

English Florists' tulips

Tulipa
Historic tulip
Liliaceae

Position
Sun

Growing conditions
Gritty soil

Plant in
Late autumn

Flowers in
Late spring

RHS H6, USDA 3–8

The pedigree of English Florists' tulips can be traced back to the first flowers grown by British gardeners John Evelyn and John Rea in the seventeenth century: since 1836, these exquisite tulips have been grown and shown by members of the Wakefield and North of England Tulip Society. At the Society's annual meetings, they are staged in the traditional way, in brown beer bottles, to best display the detail of their flowers. English Florists' tulips are divided into three colour categories – bybloemens (mauve to purple/white), roses (pink to red/white) and bizarres (orange to brown/yellow) – and each can be shown in three forms: a solid-coloured 'breeder' tulip, a 'feather', which has delicate markings to its petal edges, and a 'flame', which has a beam of contrasting colour down the petals' centre. The nuance of the markings makes them the most prized tulips grown today. In the tradition of historic florists' societies, members share these valuable bulbs among themselves. The Society is also working with Hortus Bulborum in the Netherlands to cultivate these historic tulips, and a few companies now offer a limited number for sale.

Plant bulbs in late autumn, 15 cm (6 in) deep, adding a handful of grit around them in heavier soil.

Tulipa 'James Wild'

A bizarre, broken tulip with dark red feathered markings on a yellow base. Also available in breeder form.

Height 45 cm (18 in)

Tulipa 'Lord Stanley'

Graphically flamed in red on a yellow background. A prolific flowerer and a regular award-winner at the annual show.

Height 45 cm (18 in)

Tulipa 'Mabel'

Flamed with deep rose markings on a white background. The breeder form is a rose-pink colour.

Height 40 cm (16 in)

Tulipa 'Sam Barlow'

A soft, mutable red bizarre breeder tulip, first raised around 1860.

Height 45 cm (18 in)

Tulipa 'Talisman'

Broken bybloemen with white petals flamed in purple. Also available as a breeder tulip.

Height 60 cm (18 in)

Modern Rembrandt tulips

Tulipa

Tulip

Liliaceae

Position
Sun

Growing conditions
Well-drained soil

Plant in
Late autumn

Flowers in
Mid- to late spring

RHS H6, USDA 3–8

With petals patterned and swirled in contrasting colours, the playfully striped flowers of modern Rembrandt tulips are at the brightest end of the colour spectrum. Reminiscent of the tulips in a seventeenth-century Dutch still-life painting, they capture the spirit of 'tulip mania' – when single bulbs changed hands for incredible prices – but in a reliable, affordable and easy-to-grow bulb. Good companions include pick-and-mix combinations of colourful wallflowers (*Erysimum* sp.) that bring out the eccentricity of their colours, and single late-flowering tulips in chiming or contrasting hues. Lily-flowered *Tulipa* 'Merlot' is a good match for *T.* 'Rems Favourite', flowering at the same time and highlighting its plum stripes. And *T.* 'Ballade' shares the same red-and-white colouring as *T.* 'Raspberry Ripple', which makes them another good pairing.

Late autumn is the best time to plant the bulbs, as they benefit from a cold snap after planting, which lessens the chance of the disease tulip fire. Plant 15 cm (6 in) deep with the pointed ends up in groups of eight to ten, adding grit under and around the bulbs in heavier soil.

Tulipa 'Rems Favourite'

Triumph cup-shaped tulip with violet swirls on a white background.

Height 50 cm (20 in)

Tulipa 'Burning Heart'

A Darwin hybrid that should flower reliably for several years. Long-lasting flowers with strawberry-red marbling over white.

Height 50 cm (20 in)

RHS Award of Garden Merit (AGM)

Tulipa 'Carnaval de Rio'

Triumph tulip with pretty red, orange and yellow markings on a predominantly white flower.

Height 50 cm (20 in)

Tulipa 'Estella Rijnveld'

A brightly rippled parrot type, swirled in white and red. Late flowering and good for container plantings.

Height 55 cm (22 in)

Tulipa 'Flaming Springgreen'

A Viridiflora type with green flashes over white and flecked with red. Late flowering and perennial.

Height 50 cm (20 in)

Tulipa 'Grand Perfection'

Late-flowering Triumph tulip with vanilla flowers swirled with red; the creamy colour fades to white as the season progresses. Perennial.

Height 45 cm (18 in)

RHS Award of Garden Merit (AGM)

Tulipa 'Helmar'

Triumph group. Bright red on a soft yellow base, the petals open into a broad cup shape. Long stemmed.

Height 40 cm (16 in)

RHS Award of Garden Merit (AGM)

Tulipa 'Prinses Irene'

Triumph tulip with vermilion flame markings over copper orange. Sturdy and resilient.

Height 30 cm (12 in)

RHS Award of Garden Merit (AGM)

Tulipa 'Raspberry Ripple'

Red-marbled flowers with a square shape to the petals.

Height 50 cm (20 in)

Fritillaria meleagris

Fritillaria

Snake's head fritillary

Liliaceae

Height
30 cm (12 in)

Position
Sun

Growing conditions
Damp soil that doesn't
lie wet

Plant in
Mid- to late autumn

Flowers in
Mid-spring

Perennial

RHS H5, USDA 3–8

RHS Award of Garden
Merit (AGM)

Described as a 'sombre, sinister little flower' by the gardener and writer
Vita Sackville-West in her 1927 poem 'The Land', the chequered flowers of
Fritillaria meleagris capture the imagination, crooking their necks in readiness to open in late spring. This is a useful bulb for damp soil, including in
grass as part of a meadow, thanks in part to its light and graceful foliage.
It's also a magnet for bees and other pollinators. In its favoured conditions
it will self-seed readily, even throwing up the occasional white flower. 'It has
the most delicate flower head. Its presence always makes me think that
spring is just around the corner,' says the American florist Kim Fleming.
The garden writer Kendra Wilson recommends growing it by a north-
facing doorway (sheltered and out of the sun) with cowslips (*Primula veris*),
another British native that similarly benefits from close observation.

In autumn, plant corms 20 cm (8 in) deep in damp soil, with their
pointed ends up. Water once on planting, especially if the weather is dry.
It is important to leave the foliage in place after flowering to replenish the
corms so that they will flower again the following year. Don't remove the
seedheads until they have opened and dispersed their seed in late spring
and early summer.

Fritillaria
uva-vulpis

Fritillaria

Fox's grape fritillary

Liliaceae

Height
25 cm (10 in)

Position
Sun or partial shade

Growing conditions
Gritty compost or
sharply drained soil

Plant in
Autumn

Flowers in
Mid-spring

Perennial

RHS H5, USDA 3–8

RHS Award of Garden
Merit (AGM)

A less common, but easy-to-grow small-flowered fritillary that is popular with floral artists. British florists Aesme Studio grow it as a cut flower to use with the wild tulip *Tulipa sylvestris* (p.85) and *Fritillaria michailovskyi* (p.109), where its narrow, curving stems give a 'dancing movement'. The square, nut-brown flowers have a metallic appearance above green, flat foliage. Commonly known as the fox's grape fritillary, it is widely distributed in the wild in eastern Turkey and Iran, often occupying disturbed habitats.

Bulbs are small and best grown in pots, as they need very sharp drainage. Plant three to a small container, planting them 10 cm (4 in) deep, in a gritty mix, two parts peat-free compost to one part horticultural grit, topped with an extra layer of grit to protect the flowers from getting splashed in the rain.

This fritillary is a good candidate for forcing. To force the flowers into bloom a few weeks early, keep the pot in cool, dark conditions, moving it into the light only as the first shoots appear. Otherwise, it is hardy and can be grown outside.

Fritillaria acmopetala

Fritillaria
Pointed-petal fritillary
Liliaceae

Height
25 cm (10 in)

Position
Sun or partial shade

Growing conditions
Gritty compost or sharply drained soil

Plant in
Autumn

Flowers in
Mid-spring

Perennial

RHS H4, USDA 3–8

RHS Award of Garden Merit (AGM)

Commonly, the pointed-petal fritillary, *Fritillaria acmopetala*, occupies the niche for grace and poise in an off-beat colour. Marked olive-green over muted purple, the flowers hang down from arching stems, and are slightly recurved at the tips, giving them a bell shape. 'The stems are tall with narrow arching leaves that lend it a graceful profile,' notes British regenerative gardener Alison Jenkins. In the courtyard garden at the Garden Museum in London, it is displayed in terracotta pots so that visitors can observe its flowers closely.

The bulbs are small and need very sharp drainage. Add a layer of grit to the base of a pot filled with gritty loam-based compost, two parts peat-free to one part horticultural grit. Plant bulbs 10 cm (4 in) deep, five per pot, at close spacing and with an extra topping of grit to stop the flowers from getting dirtied when it rains. Water sparingly once the flowers appear.

Fritillaria michailovskyi

Fritillaria

Michailovskyi's fritillary, Michael's flower

Liliaceae

Height
25 cm (10 in)

Position
Sun or partial shade

Growing conditions
Gritty compost or sharply drained soil

Plant in
Autumn

Flowers in
Mid-spring

Perennial

RHS H5, USDA 3–8

The smaller-flowered fritillaries, including Michael's flower (*Fritillaria michailovskyi*), are often best grown in containers in sunny spots, as their flowers are easily missed in the garden. At Sissinghurst Castle Garden in Kent, *F. michailovskyi* grows in troughs in the Top Courtyard; the former deputy head gardener Joshua Sparkes describes them as 'slightly rugged...creating a strong presence, instantly drawing your attention'. The flowers are plum-coloured with mustard tips and an iridescent sheen, beautifully set off by greyish-green foliage. Native to Turkey, where it grows on stony, mountainous slopes, *F. michailovskyi* needs a dry summer after flowering.

Plant bulbs 10 cm (4 in) deep, five to a small pot, using a gritty mix, two parts loam-based compost to one part horticultural grit, topped with a further layer of grit to stop the flowers from getting marked in the rain. After flowering, keep the pots somewhere warm, dry and sheltered until you bring them out again the following autumn.

Fritillaria imperialis

Fritillaria

Crown imperial, Kaiser's crown

Liliaceae

Height	**Flowers in**
1 m (39 in)	Mid- to late spring
Position	**Perennial**
Sun	RHS H7, USDA 3–8
Growing conditions	**RHS Award of Garden**
Damp, well-drained soil	**Merit (AGM)**
Plant in	
Early autumn to early winter	

The tall and imposing outline of *Fritillaria imperialis* can make it tricky to place in the garden. Giant flowerheads nose up in early spring with up to 12 brick-orange flowers per stem. At his private garden, Allt-y-Bela, in Monmouthshire, Wales, British garden designer Arne Maynard highlights the flowers' rich orange tones, bold form and dark, smoky stems by growing them at the foot of a clipped beech hedge to coordinate with the copper-orange juvenile foliage in spring.

Native to the mountainous regions of Turkey, western Iran and eastwards to Kashmir, *F. imperialis* benefits from being planted in deep loamy soil that doesn't sit wet. In autumn, plant bulbs 30cm (12 in) deep, adding a handful of grit or leaf mould around each one. Plant the bulbs on their side so that water doesn't accumulate in their stem holes. Space them in irregular patterns to imitate their natural distribution.

Fritillaria persica

Fritillaria

Persian lily

Syn. *Fritillaria arabica*

Liliaceae

Height
1 m (39 in)

Position
Sun

Growing conditions
Any soil

Plant in
Early to mid-autumn

Flowers in
Early to mid-spring

Perennial

RHS H4, USDA 3–8

RHS Award of Garden Merit (AGM)

A tall plant with a small footprint, *Fritillaria persica* is a stylish way to add height to the garden in mid-spring. Its flower spike is a staggered arrangement of blooms that are dusky purple on the petal reverse and brighter inside, with striking yellow stamens. The flowers register easily, held clear of their grey-green foliage.

Native to the scrubland and rocky slopes of Turkey and the Middle East, the best garden combinations reference this heritage, combining it with tall grasses and flowers, such as snowy woodrush (*Luzula nivalis*), that have a wilder aesthetic. The Spanish landscape architect Miguel Urquijo notes that it will readily self-sow in sharply drained soil, with new seedlings taking four or five years to reach flowering size.

The bulbs have a papery tunic and are big but fragile; they bruise easily and need gentle handling. Plant them 20 cm (8 in) deep in a sunny spot, in autumn or spring, adding grit underneath and around each bulb to ensure it doesn't sit wet.

Ornithogalum umbellatum

Ornithogalum

Milk flower, common star of Bethlehem

Asparagaceae

Height
20 cm (8 in)

Position
Sun or partial shade

Growing conditions
Any soil

Plant in
Early to late autumn

Flowers in
Mid- to late spring

Perennial

RHS H5, USDA 3–8

Adaptable and easy, this diminutive early milk flower is a lovely thing naturalized in grass, offering good forage for early flying bees and other pollinators. 'It has been known to spread a little too enthusiastically in some locales,' notes Charlie Harpur, head gardener at Britain's flagship rewilding estate, Knepp in West Sussex. 'I've always had a soft spot for it, but it should not be allowed to run freely in the border.' (In the United States it is an aggressive grower and potentially invasive in some locales.) Its small, bright, white starry flowers are marked in pale green and held in loose clusters atop narrow, grass-like foliage.

In autumn, use the blade of a spade to make slits in the grass, 8 cm (3 in) deep, and add a little grit. Plant bulbs 10 cm (4 in) apart, 10 per square metre (9 per square yard), push back the turf and gently firm down. After flowering, wait a minimum of six weeks before mowing the grass, to allow the foliage to replenish the bulb for the following year.

Tropaeolum tricolor

Tropaeolum

Chilean nasturtium, flame creeper, three-coloured nasturtium

Tropaeolaceae

Height
1.2 m (47 in)

Position
Sun

Growing conditions
Pot culture, loam-based compost

Plant in
Late summer

Flowers in
Mid- to late spring

Perennial

RHS H2, USDA 8–10

RHS Award of Garden Merit (AGM)

A lesser-known but brilliantly coloured climbing plant that shoots in autumn, climbs during winter, flowers in spring and is dormant by summer. Its ascent is early and nicely timed, and the flowers a pretty vignette of rich red, plum and yellow. Native to the cloud forests of Chile, it is easy, long flowering and adaptable. It is a favourite of plantsperson and award-winning nurseryperson Chris Ireland-Jones, formerly of Avon Bulbs in the UK.

Plant the small tubers individually, 8 cm (3 in) deep in big pots of peat-free compost, providing support for the stems as they grow using a scaffold of pea-sticks from the garden. Post-flowering and after a dry summer rest, refresh the compost each autumn.

Allium siculum

Allium

Nectaroscordum, Sicilian honey garlic

Syn. *Nectaroscordum siculum*

Amaryllidaceae

Height
1.2 m (47 in)

Position
Sun or partial shade

Growing conditions
Well-drained soil

Plant in
Early to late autumn

Flowers in
Late spring to early summer

Perennial

RHS H5, USDA 5–8b

A type of pendulous allium and an easy ticket to wildness, with dangling, bell-shaped florets in greenish white, boldly marked with plum. It is wonderful in measured amounts, studding low, bunching grasses such as feather grass (*Stipa tenuissima*) or other late spring-flowering umbels, such as bishop's weed (*Ammi visnaga*) and white laceflower (*Orlaya grandiflora*), where its flowers register heavily among their more gossamer forms (see pp.118–19).

Pollinators animate its flowers in early summer. After pollination, individual florets reach back skywards and turn pointed at their tips. When it is happy with its spot, it is an enthusiastic self-seeder.

In autumn, plant bulbs 15 cm (6 in) deep, 15 cm (6 in) apart, with their pointed ends upwards, adding a little grit under and around each bulb.

Opposite:

Allium siculum with *Salvia nemerosa* in a British garden designed by Penelope Hobhouse

Allium tripedale

Allium

Nectaroscordum, eastern honey garlic

Syn. *Nectaroscordum tripedale*

Amaryllidaceae

Height
1.5 m (59 in)

Position
Sun or partial shade

Growing conditions
Well-drained soil

Plant in
Early to late autumn

Flowers in
Late spring to early summer

Perennial

RHS H5, USDA 5–9

A tall, choice relative of the popular flowering bulb nectaroscordum (*Allium siculum*, p.116), with the same drooping florets and beautifully unusual colouring. The colour of the flowers can vary a little, with some a little darker than others. The flowers are densely packed on their stems and open incrementally before eventually reaching back skywards as they are pollinated. This allium was used by British designer Sarah Price in combination with *A. siculum* and airy *Agrostis capillaris* grass in her colourful Benton End-inspired garden for RHS Chelsea flower show in 2023 (see pp.118–19). In the courtyard garden at Hauser and Wirth Somerset, by Dutch designer and plantsperson Piet Oudolf, it grows alongside shooting star (*Dodecatheon jeffreyi*), spurge (*Euphorbia griffithii* 'Dixter') and moor grass (*Sesleria autumnalis*) as part of a coolly textural planting.

In autumn, plant bulbs 15 cm (6 in) deep and 15 cm (6 in) apart with their pointed ends upwards. *A. tripedale*'s flowers are sterile and don't set seed, so this form is less promiscuous than *A. siculum*. Instead, it will increase underground to form clumps gradually.

Previous pages:
Allium tripedale and *A. siculum* in a wild planting with *Ammi visnaga* in the Nurture Landscapes Garden at RHS Chelsea flower show, designed by Sarah Price

Asphodelus albus

Asphodelus

White asphodel

Asphodelaceae

Height
1.5 m (59 in)

Position
Sun

Growing conditions
Well-drained soil

Plant in
Late summer

Flowers in
Late spring to midsummer

Perennial

RHS H6, USDA 6–9

The bulb to reach for for height and architecture in a gravel or sand garden, with tall flower spikes that rise from a tight whorl of grey-ish-green foliage. British designer Conrad Batten, who is known for his wilder-style planting, recommends mixing it with shrubby herbs such as rosemary (*Salvia rosmarinus*), thyme (*Thymus* sp.) and lavender (*Lavandula* sp.). It also goes well with *Artemisia*, shrubby euphorbias and grasses. The petals of each small floret are marked with a pinkish-brown line down the middle, which gives the flower spikes an overall pinky tone with a toffee-coloured tip. It grows wild in the Mediterranean in free-draining soil, where it is very long flowering.

Plant tubers in late summer, 10 cm (4 in) deep, in sharply drained soil, adding a handful of grit underneath and watering once on plant-ing. It increases readily underground, giving the opportunity for lifting and splitting big clumps in winter.

Benton irises

Iris

Tall bearded iris

Iridaceae

Position
Sun

Growing conditions
Well-drained soil

Plant in
Late summer to
autumn, spring

Flowers in
Late spring

Perennial

RHS H6, USDA 3–8

Iris 'Benton Nigel'

Violet flowers with a
vibrant top note and
a Parma violet scent,
named after Nigel Scott,
gardener at Benton End.

Height 90 cm (35 in)

**RHS Award of Garden
Merit (AGM)**

Benton irises are notable for their grace of form and complexity of colour. Between 1934 and 1960 the artist/gardener Cedric Morris (1889–1982) raised thousands of bearded iris seedlings in his garden at Benton End in Suffolk, throwing iris parties timed to coincide with and celebrate the opening of his flowers. Making crosses between pairs of tall bearded irises, he deliberately bred for nuanced colour and stitched or stippled markings, known as plicata, in contrast to the background colour of the petals, which are known as standards (the top three petals of each flower) and falls (the bottom three). In all, Morris named over 90 cultivars, selected with the trained eye of an artist for their well-spaced flowers, which are free from frill or flounce. Benton irises are the first choice for many garden designers working today, including Julian and Isabel Bannerman and Dan Pearson. Many are also now cultivated in the Sussex garden of Sarah Cook (pp.124–5), who holds the Plant Heritage Historic Collection of Iris (Sir Cedric Morris introductions).

Irises need full sun to grow well, and do best without competition. Plant rhizomes in midsummer in gritty soil, keeping the top third of the rhizome clear of the surface, and water on planting.

Iris 'Benton Arundel'

One of the most unusually coloured of all the Benton irises: fragrant plum-brown-and-white flowers with brown plicata markings on the falls. The bold colours contrast with the glaucous, sword-shaped foliage.

Height 50 cm (20 in)

Iris 'Benton Caramel'

Rich brown with hints of red and apricot in the throat.

Height 50 cm (20 in)

Iris 'Benton Menace'

Bruised purple flowers with good plicata patterning and a contrasting yellow beard. Good for scent, too. Said to be named after one of Cedric Morris's cats!

Height 50 cm (20 in)

Iris 'Benton Nutkin'

Russet with a trace of violet and brown plicata markings on the falls. A particular favourite of Cedric Morris himself.

Height 50 cm (20 in)

Iris 'Benton Olive'

Mutable, yellow-brown flowers with a hint of violet and a contrasting orange beard. Named after Olive Murrell, who sold Morris's irises at her Kent nursery.

Height 50 cm (20 in)

Iris 'Benton Pearl'

Milk-white-and-yellow flowers with a yellow beard, making a showy display in early summer.

Height 50 cm (20 in)

Iris 'Benton Susan'

Tawny brown flowers with stippled violet markings.

Height 50 cm (20 in)

Iris 'Storrington'

Syn. *Iris* 'Benton Storrington' Rich plum-coloured standards with deep plum falls. The plicata markings on the falls echo the colour in the standards.

Height 50 cm (20 in)

Dichelostemma capitatum

Dichelostemma

Blue dicks

Asparagaceae

Height
50 cm (20 in)

Position
Sun

Growing conditions
Well-drained soil

Plant in
Early autumn

Flowers in
Late spring to early summer

Perennial

RHS H5, USDA 7b–11

A summer-dormant corm that is never overwhelming and is happy in the company of bunching grasses. Growing wild in the low chaparral landscapes and grasslands of California, where rain might not fall for several months, it is suited to a dry spot and works well as part of gravel or sand gardens. California-based garden designer Bernard Trainor notes that 'it emerges from our grassland and oak savannah designed eco-types, intermingling with other early-flowering wild-flowers such as Californian varieties of poppies, yarrow and lupins.' The stems, he adds, 'twist their way through the indigenous grasses, attracting bees, butterflies and hummingbirds'. The ultraviolet 'bee blue' colour of the flowers means they are easily spotted from on the wing, and are a good source of pollen and nectar. Since the flowers do not open all at once on the same plant, it is in bloom for several weeks. Leave seedpods in place after flowering and, in favoured conditions, volunteer seedlings will appear in spring.

Plant the corms 10 cm (4 in) deep 2.5 cm (1 in) apart, adding grit under and around each one.

Previous pages:
Benton irises in the garden of British gardener Sarah Cook, who rescued them from obscurity and is the holder of the Plant Heritage Historic Collection of Iris (Sir Cedric Morris introductions)

Scilla peruviana

Scilla

Giant squill, Portuguese squill

Syn. *Oncostema peruviana*

Asparagaceae

Height
30 cm (12 in)

Position
Full sun or dappled shade

Growing conditions
Well-drained soil

Plant in
Mid-autumn

Flowers in
Late spring to early summer

Perennial

RHS H4, USDA 7b–10

Commonly named Portuguese squill, this is a favourite bulb of Dutch designer and plantsperson Piet Oudolf, used among late-flowering perennials in his private garden, Hummelo, in the Netherlands. Found in the wild on roadside verges and in open woodland in dappled light, it is the essence of a Mediterranean bulb with a form, colour and habit that are quintessentially warm climate. Its near-metallic flowers are brilliant blue; the dark green, strappy leaves are almost evergreen in a temperate climate and given summer heat it is reliably perennial. The UK-based garden designer Manoj Malde recommends it as an easy bulb for gardening beginners, saying, 'It will grow well in containers, borders and gravel or coastal gardens.'

Unlike most bulbs that dwell underground, *Scilla peruviana* should be planted shallowly, keeping the nose of each bulb just proud of the soil. Add a handful of grit under and around each one to ensure it doesn't sit wet, and choose a sunny spot to give it a warm summer bake, keeping watering to a minimum.

Summer

Camassia quamash

Camassia leichtlinii 'Alba'

Camassia leichtlinii subsp.
  suksdorfii 'Maybelle'

Gladiolus tristis

Ornithogalum pyrenaicum

Ornithogalum magnum
  'Moskou'

Ornithogalum ponticum
  'Sochi'

Gladiolus communis
  subsp. byzantinus

Triteleia 'Rudy'

Scilla hyacinthoides
  'Blue Arrow'

Anemone coronaria
  'Bordeaux'

Allium 'Pink Jewel'

Allium obliquum

Allium 'Mont Blanc'

Allium angulosum

Allium schubertii

Allium atropurpureum

Allium 'Summer Drummer'

Allium sphaerocephalon

Gladiolus papilio

Gladiolus 'Ruby'

Lilium pardalinum var.
  giganteum

Lilium pomponium

Martagon lilies

Giant-flowered lilies

Lilium regale

Tulbaghia violacea

Tulbaghia violacea
  'Silver Lace'

Liatris spicata 'Alba'

Gladiolus 'Nathalie'

Gladiolus murielae

Bessera elegans

Tritonia disticha subsp.
  rubrolucens

Cardiocrinum cordatum
  var. glehnii

Acis autumnalis

By contrast with the green of spring, summer-flowering bulbs are in competition with the garden at full reach. Think of them as colourful and ephemeral ingredients in successional, layered combinations. Many are at their best planted in irregular patterns that replicate their habits in nature: pushing up among the emergent foliage of later-flowering perennials; woven between bunching, warm-season grasses where their foliage is easily lost after flowering; or providing a change of scale and shape as a component in super-layered planting.

At the Hepworth Wakefield in West Yorkshire, in the garden designed by Tom Stuart-Smith, brilliant white *Ornithogalum magnum* 'Moskou' is a perfect foil for the colours of adjacent plants. At Great Dixter in East Sussex, *Gladiolus communis* subsp. *byzantinus* makes a good mingler among cow parsley (*Anthriscus sylvestris*) and *Verbascum*, following forget-me-nots (*Myosotis*) and violets; elsewhere *Gladiolus papilio* adds easy height and weight to feather grass (*Stipa tenuissima*).

Alliums are as useful for their seedheads post-bloom as they are for their summer flowers. Sturdy and architectural, the seedheads echo the shape of the original flowers and cast shadows in the play of light. There is an allium for every outdoor space, from hefty-flowered, pale *Allium* 'Mont Blanc' to pleasingly unkempt *A. obliquum* and the small, window-box and pollinator-friendly *A. angulosum*.

The fat new shoots of summer lilies are packed full of promise and excitement. Martagon lilies are a colourful twist in dappled light, while in full sun and ticking heat the huge, stamen-bossed flowers of *Lilium regale* hang heavily with scent. In the run-up to the summer solstice, the light is on their side.

Camassia quamash

Camassia

Indian hyacinth,
bear's grass, camas

Syn. *Camassia esculeta* Lindl.,
Camassia teapeae

Asparagaceae

Height
60 cm (24 in)

Position
Sun or partial shade

Growing conditions
Damp, humus-rich soil

Plant in
Early to mid-autumn

Flowers in
Late spring to early summer

Perennial

RHS H4, USDA 4–9

A small, bright camassia that is easily snuck into the border between the emergent foliage of later-flowering plants. This is a good companion for the freckled spires of foxgloves (*Digitalis* sp.) that flower at the same time and are a similar shape, and similarly benefit from the damp soil in dappled shade. Alternatively, threaded through cow parsley (*Anthriscus sylvestris*) and Baltic parsley (*Cenolophium denudatum*), it makes an uplifting early summer combination that hints at a wild place. 'The dark blue flowers are loved by bees and need very little attention,' says British landscape architect Marian Boswall.

The bulbs are small and round. Plant them in autumn, 10–15 cm (4–6 in) deep, with their pointed ends up. Water after planting, particularly if the weather is dry. A very reliable bulb that will last for years in the garden and, given the right conditions, increase its numbers by self-seeding.

Camassia leichtlinii 'Alba'

Camassia

Large camas, Californian white-flowered quamash

Syn. *Camassia leichtlinii* subsp. *leichtlinii* 'Alba'

Asparagaceae

Height
90 cm (35 in)

Position
Sun or partial shade

Growing conditions
Damp soil

Plant in
Early to mid-autumn

Flowers in
Late spring to early summer

Perennial

RHS H4, USDA 3–9

Following pages:
A succession of spring bulbs, including snowdrops, scilla, muscari, narcissi and camassia, in the topiary meadow at Caisson gardens, near Bath

An indispensable bulb for damp soil in sun or dappled shade where few others thrive, and the go-to bulb for a dynamic meadow, *Camassia leichtlinii* 'Alba' is useful in long grass, including under trees, where the opening of its flowers coincides beautifully with the bursting of the blossom. The flowers hover and hold their own, and the narrow foliage is easily lost in the grass after flowering. 'Tall and sturdy, this camassia is planted in our Stone Orchard; it pulls the eye up as it nods gently in the breeze above the meadow grasses and it almost glows in the early evening light', says James McGrath, head gardener of a private estate in Connecticut, designed by Dan Pearson.

In his front garden in the city of Sheffield, British designer Nigel Dunnett grows *C. leichtlinii* 'Alba' in a pretty combination with a purple *Iris sibirica* 'Mrs Rowe' and pink *Persicaria bistort* as part of a rain garden that absorbs the water runoff redirected from the roof of his house.

Plant bulbs 10–15 cm (4–6 in) deep in autumn. In favoured conditions, it will increase its numbers by self-seeding enthusiastically.

Camassia leichtlinii subsp. *suksdorfii* 'Maybelle'

Camassia

Camas

Asparagaceae

Height
60 cm (24 in)

Position
Sun or partial shade

Growing conditions
Humus-rich soil

Plant in
Early to late autumn

Flowers in
Late spring to early summer

Perennial

RHS H4, USDA 3–9

Worth seeking out over other named varieties of camassia for its refinement and poise, *Camassia leichtlinii* subsp. *suksdorfii* 'Maybelle' has clear blue flowers with bright yellow middles on darkened stems. An essential bulb for damp soil in a sunny spot, it is a favourite of award-winning nurseryperson Chris Ireland-Jones, formerly of Avon Bulbs in the UK, who notes, 'the flowers are the bluest of blue, where other cultivars tend towards purple, and are a degree or two more widely spaced apart. The foliage is markedly narrow, so it continues to look good even as the flowers fade.'

Plant bulbs in autumn, 15 cm (6 in) deep, with their pointed ends up, and water once on planting, particularly if the weather is dry. The flowers are sterile and don't self-seed, so unlike other camassia it doesn't overreach its spot. Leave the foliage in place after flowering to replenish the bulb for the following year.

Gladiolus tristis

Gladiolus

Marsh Afrikaner, wintergreen

Iridaceae

Height
90 cm (35 in)

Position
Sun

Growing conditions
Well-drained soil

Plant in
Mid- to late spring

Flowers in
Late spring to early summer

Perennial

RHS H4, USDA 8–11

'The tall blades of *Gladiolus tristis* are visible in autumn and need a sheltered corner to survive winter unscathed,' says British designer Dan Pearson. In his private garden, Hillside, near Bath in southwest England, they abut a corrugated-iron fence, where they stand tall throughout the winter, in readiness to flower in the months ahead. This is a delicate and wand-like gladiolus with pale yellow flowers that open progressively up narrow stems in late spring and early summer. 'Plants that strain and topple for the light will need the support of twiggy stems pushed into the soil around them,' notes Pearson. This is a job that is best done in autumn, as the first shoots appear. Early flowering, *G. tristis* is dormant by July.

Plant corms in a sheltered spot in spring, 10 cm (4 in) deep in humus-rich soil that doesn't sit wet.

Ornithogalum pyrenaicum

Ornithogalum

Bath asparagus, spiked star of Bethlehem

Asparagaceae

Height
50 cm (20 in)

Position
Sun or partial shade

Growing conditions
Well-drained soil

Plant in
Early to late autumn

Flowers in
Early summer

Perennial

RHS H6, USDA 6–7

Ornithogalum pyrenaicum grows wild in the southwest of England. Delicate in bud and much like the grass itself in colour, tall spires of pale green flowers run up the stems in early summer. 'It is often found in the company of bluebells, and it is happy in cool grassland or in a shady border with *Digitalis* (foxgloves) and martagon lilies,' says British landscape designer Dan Pearson. In order to produce enough plants for a flow in the garden, Pearson recommends growing it from seed. 'The four or five years to flowering size feel like nothing once you have them in relay and the first of the years behind you.'

Sow seeds under cover in autumn, scattering them lightly on the surface of pots of gritty compost with enough room between the seeds for the seedlings to develop their first true leaves before they need transplanting. Cover with a little more compost and keep outside.

Ornithogalum magnum 'Moskou'

Ornithogalum

Giant star of Bethlehem

Asparagaceae

Height
60 cm (24 in)

Position
Sun

Growing conditions
Well-drained soil

Plant in
Early to mid-autumn

Flowers in
Early summer

Perennial

RHS H5, USDA 3a–8b

Following pages:

The white spires of summer-flowering bulb *Ornithogalum magnum* 'Moskou' add height to the planting at the Hepworth Wakefield Garden in Yorkshire, designed by Tom Stuart-Smith

White-flowered *Ornithogalum magnum* 'Moskou' 'makes everything around it shine a little bit brighter', says Katy Merrington, cultural gardener at the Hepworth Wakefield in Yorkshire, where it flowers, tall and luminous (see overleaf), among purple *Salvia nemorosa* 'Caradonna' (sage), blue *Amsonia tabernaemontana* (amsonia) and acid-green *Euphorbia wallichii* (spurge) as part of the complementary combination conceived by British designer Tom Stuart-Smith. It is an ideal candidate for layered planting, making adjacent colours seem far livelier than they would without it. Chunky in bud, after flowering the individual blooms linger on the stems as smoky tails, creating late summer interest.

In autumn, plant bulbs 10 cm (4 in) deep, adding a little grit with each one and nestling them in between summer-flowering perennial plants. Post-flower, leave the foliage on the bulb so that it can photosynthesize and replenish its resources for the following summer.

Ornithogalum ponticum 'Sochi'

Ornithogalum

Star of Bethlehem

Asparagaceae

Height
60 cm (24 in)

Position
Sun

Growing conditions
Gritty compost

Plant in
Early to mid-autumn

Flowers in
Early summer

Perennial

RHS H4, USDA 5–9

'There are so many great *Ornithogalum* in cultivation, all of them fantastic in pots,' notes Matt Collins, head gardener at the Garden Museum in London. 'Having experimented with a few, *O. ponticum* "Sochi" is probably the best of the bunch: late and long flowering, tall, reliable and spectacularly brightly petalled.' A Russian woodlander, it has narrow flowerheads packed with small white flowers that are marked green on their petals and open from the base up.

In autumn, plant six bulbs to a 20 cm (8 in) pot, planting them 15 cm (6 in) deep, in a gritty compost mix, two parts peat-free compost to one part horticultural grit; top with an extra layer of grit to reduce watering. After flowering, leave the foliage in situ to replenish resources in the bulb for the following year. It is also an excellent cut flower, with a long vase-life.

Gladiolus communis subsp. byzantinus

Gladiolus

Byzantine gladiolus

Iridaceae

Height
60 cm (24 in)

Position
Sun

Growing conditions
Well-drained soil

Plant in
Early to late autumn

Flowers in
Early to midsummer

Perennial

RHS H5, USDA 7–10

The garden at Great Dixter in East Sussex has a reputation for being loose. 'The intense, magenta-pink flowers of *Gladiolus communis* subsp. *byzantinus* make it a good mingler among perennials,' says head gardener Fergus Garrett, who grows it among thistle-like cardoons (*Cynara cardunculus*), cow parsley (*Anthriscus sylvestris*) and ladybird poppies (*Papaver commutatum* 'Ladybird') as part of a colourful combination. Its narrow flower spikes are equally at home in Great Dixter's Front Meadow, where they have naturalized in the long grass jostling alongside buttercups (*Ranunculus acris*) and ox-eye daisies (*Leucanthemum vulgare*). Tall, arching flower spikes and thin, flat, upright foliage mean it does not squeeze its neighbours out.

In autumn, plant corms 10 cm (4 in) deep, with their pointed ends up, adding a spadeful of grit to the planting holes. The corms are borderline hardy in temperate climates, so a heap of protective compost over the top of their spot in winter is a good idea. Leave the foliage in place after flowering: it is easily lost in grass or among the leaves of nearby plants.

Triteleia 'Rudy'

Triteleia

Triplet lily

Asparagaceae

Height
45 cm (18 in)

Position
Sun

Growing conditions
Well-drained soil

Plant in
Early to mid-spring

Flowers in
Early summer

Perennial

RHS H4, USDA 5–9

A pretty flower with elfin grace that is a good choice for a rubbly soil or for sand plantings as part of a subtly colourful palette. It will cope with the increasingly dry summers and wet but milder winters we are experiencing as a consequence of climate change. A Californian native, there is little left of its foliage at the point of flowering. Umbels unfurl at the tips of narrow, upright stems, and each white petal is marked down the middle with a diffused violet stripe. Umbels are the predominant flower shape in the natural landscape, and *Triteleia* associates easily with plants from the arid environment from which it came, such as *Dichelostemma capitatum* (blue dicks, p.126) or *Mathiasella bupleuroides* 'Green Dream'. This is a lovely, lesser-known plant and extremely long flowering. It is hardy and reliably perennial.

In spring, plant corms 8 cm (3 in) deep in gritty soil, with the pointed ends upwards.

Scilla hyacinthoides 'Blue Arrow'

Scilla

Hyacinth squill

Asparagaceae

Height
70 cm (28 in)

Position
Sun or partial shade

Growing conditions
Well-drained soil

Plant in
Early to mid-autumn

Flowers in
Early summer

Perennial

RHS H6, USDA 7–10

'The tall, pyramidal flowers of *Scilla hyacinthoides* "Blue Arrow" are beautiful when used under pines with warm-season grasses, hovering in the space before the rush of high-summer growth,' says British garden designer Conrad Batten, who is recognized for his sustainable and painterly plant combinations. At their best when planted in irregular patterns to emulate their self-seeding and distribution patterns in nature, the light blue flowers are well spaced on their stems, which are darker blue, and held above scant, dark green foliage. The flowers register lightly and the foliage is easily lost in the grass after flowering. This plant thrives in sun or dappled shade and is ideal for naturalizing, benefiting from the lack of moisture that is a consequence of the trees' roots.

Plant bulbs 20 cm (8 in) deep in autumn, using a trowel or hori hori to winkle them in. Choose a site where they will get plenty of sun and where they can be allowed to naturalize.

Anemone coronaria 'Bordeaux'

Anemone

Garden anemone, Irish anemone, poppy windflower

Ranunculaceae

Height
45 cm (18 in)

Position
Sun

Growing conditions
Gritty compost, protect from frost

Plant in
Mid-spring

Flowers in
Early summer

Perennial

RHS H5, USDA 8–10

Sometimes mistaken for a poppy due to its colouring and the poppy-like form of its flowers, this is a glorious wildflower in olive groves in the Mediterranean, and plant breeders have taken advantage of its variable nature to create new cultivars in a rich, vibrant palette of colours. Of these, nurseryperson Joe Sharman recommends *Anemone coronaria* 'Bordeaux' for its huge, rich velvety-purple flowers with a spectacular blue eye. *A. coronaria* grows well in large terracotta pots and is easily forced into early flowering indoors, making it popular with contemporary floral artists.

Soak the twig-like corms in tepid water for three or four hours ahead of planting to encourage them to start more easily into growth. Plant several corms to a large pot, in a gritty mix, two parts compost to one part horticultural grit, laying them horizontally, 1 cm (½ in) deep and with a deep root run below. Water once on planting, then sparingly but more often as the foliage and flowers appear. After flowering, the corms can be transplanted outside into the garden, where they will flower annually in summer.

Allium 'Pink Jewel'

Allium

Ornamental onion

Amaryllidaceae

Height
50 cm (20 in)

Position
Sun

Growing conditions
Well-drained soil

Plant in
Early to late autumn

Flowers in
Late spring to early summer

Perennial

RHS H6, USDA 4a–10

This boxy-shaped allium is a favourite of Dutch designer Piet Oudolf, who chooses it for its sturdy seedheads as much as for its true pink flowers. At Vitra Campus Garden, Weil am Rhein, Germany, Oudolf uses it in combination with prairie dropseed (*Sporobolus heterolepis*) and flowering sage (*Salvia* sp.), as well as growing it in his own garden, Hummelo, in the Netherlands. Useful at every stage in its lifecycle, it has architectural green buds that give way to densely packed, pink-petalled flowers, each with a round, green middle, eventually evolving into bobbled seedheads.

In autumn, plant bulbs 15 cm (6 in) deep, irregularly spaced to emulate the patterns of nature, adding a handful of grit under and around each bulb. It will increase readily underground, gradually forming clumps. Leave the foliage in place after flowering to replenish the bulbs for the following year. The seedheads last on the plant throughout winter.

Allium obliquum

Allium

Lopsided onion

Syn. *Allium ramosum* Jacq.

Amaryllidaceae

Height
70 cm (28 in)

Position
Sun

Growing conditions
Any soil

Plant in
Early to late autumn

Flowers in
Early summer

Perennial

RHS H4, USDA 4–8

An enjoyably unkempt allium on account of its asymmetrical, greenish-yellow flowerheads and the quirky line of its stems. Just before breaking, the buds tilt downwards and the flowers open in the space made by the crook of their stems. 'It is easily woven through groups of perennials, with the flowers wonderfully set off by the glaucous, slightly twisted foliage,' notes British plantsperson Jonny Bruce. In her 2023 RHS Chelsea flower garden celebrating the artist Cedric Morris (see p.122), it was used by designer Sarah Price as part of a palette of painterly plants alongside *Allium siculum* (p.116), *A. tripedale* (p.120) and the grass *Melica altissima* 'Alba'. Native to eastern Europe and central Asia, it gently self-seeds in its favoured conditions of sun and sharp drainage.

Plant bulbs in autumn, 15 cm (6 in) deep, spaced in irregular patterns. It will tolerate heavier soils.

Opposite:
Spheres of yellow flowers on tall stems of the perennial *Allium obliquum* add interest and rhythm to a layered border planting at Malverleys garden in Hampshire

Allium 'Mont Blanc'

Allium

Ornamental onion

Amaryllidaceae

Height
1.1 m (43 in)

Position
Sun

Growing conditions
Well-drained soil

Plant in
Early to mid-autumn

Flowers in
Early summer

Perennial

RHS H5, USDA 4–8

RHS Award of Garden Merit (AGM)

With its hefty, creamy white flowers, no bulb better captures the low light of early summer. Its flowers are huge, but leavened by their colour, so they retain an air of wildness. It is lovely scattered through emergent grasses that are studded with wildflowers, or with wilder-looking forms of cultivated plants, such as *Verbascum phoeniceum* 'Violetta'. In the gently shifting community of plants in the flagship rewilded walled garden at the Knepp Estate in West Sussex, it flowers as a ghost of the kitchen garden that once occupied the site, fitting easily into the wild aesthetic.

Plant bulbs in autumn, 20 cm (8 in) deep, in a site where the flowers will be in sun when they open. Because the flowers are large, use fewer than you might think and space them widely. After flowering, leave the foliage on the bulb to replenish it for the following summer. It forms clumps and will increase in number each year.

Allium angulosum

Allium

Mouse garlic

Syn. *Allium acutangulum*

Amaryllidaceae

Height
60 cm (24 in)

Position
Sun

Growing conditions
Any soil

Plant in
Early to mid-autumn

Flowers in
Early to midsummer

Perennial

RHS H6, USDA 4–8

A small-flowered allium that is pale green in bud and opens to near-spherical rose-pink flowers, *Allium angulosum* 'doesn't need a very sunny spot and it doesn't mind being overshadowed', notes the gardener and writer Alys Fowler. 'It is good for window boxes and, my goodness, it is delicious. I like to eat all parts of this plant, including the bulbs.' The flowers deepen in colour as they age, and by midsummer flowers and seedheads are held simultaneously on the same plant. The flowers are sterile but popular with pollinators. *A.* 'Millennium' (syn. *A. angulosum* tall form) is taller and has slightly bigger flowers.

Plant bulbs 15 cm (6 in) deep in a loam-based mix, two parts compost to one part horticultural grit, topped with an extra layer of grit to keep watering to a minimum.

Allium schubertii

Allium

Ornamental onion, Schubert's allium

Amaryllidaceae

Height
60 cm (24 in)

Position
Sun

Growing conditions
Well-drained soil

Plant in
Early to mid-autumn

Flowers in
Early to midsummer

Perennial

RHS H4, USDA 5–11

An eccentrically flowered allium with giant flowerheads that are made up of flowers on stems of different lengths. Prettily coloured, the blooms are washed mauve and green. The seedheads are also of particular merit, repeating the shape of the original flowers to cast well-defined shadows in winter. Its architectural outline makes this a popular plant with garden designers, and it is often used nestled in among summer-flowering perennials that pick up its summery colours, such as *Geranium* 'Brookside', the violet-flowered woodland sage *Salvia nemorosa* 'Amethyst', and feather grass (*Stipa tenuissima*).

In autumn, plant bulbs 15 cm (6 in) deep, adding a handful of horticultural grit with each one, and a minimum of 25 cm (10 in) apart to ensure the flowers don't overcrowd one another when they are fully open. Among alliums, this one is particular about having sharp drainage. After flowering, leave the foliage in place to replenish the bulb's resources for the following year. It will increase in number every year.

Allium atropurpureum

Allium

Ornamental onion, very dark-purple allium

Syn. *Allium nigrum* var. *atropurpureum*

Amaryllidaceae

Height
1 m (39 in)

Position
Sun

Growing conditions
Well-drained soil

Plant in
Early to mid-autumn

Flowers in
Early to midsummer

Perennial

RHS H5, USDA 5–8b

'This Balkan native is about as exquisite as it gets,' says British garden designer Cleve West, who recommends it for planting in a gravel garden, where, given some space, its blackcurrant-coloured flowers will spangle herbs, sub-shrubs and low, bunching grasses. The flowers are easy to read: hemispherical, up to 5 cm (2 in) across and held on vertical stems. In common with others in its family, *A. atropurpureum* has long-lasting seedheads that are not much of a departure in shape from their flowers and are brought to life in the play of autumn light.

In autumn, plant bulbs 15 cm (6 in) deep, with enough space between them to allow you to appreciate the half-domed form of the flowers. After flowering, leave the foliage on the bulb for a minimum of six weeks to replenish for the following summer. Unlike most alliums, *A. atropurpureum* can be slow to increase underground, but is easily forgiven for its intensity of colour.

Allium 'Summer Drummer'

Allium

Allium 'Summer Drummer'

Amaryllidaceae

Height
2 m (79 in)

Position
Sun

Growing conditions
Well-drained soil

Plant in
Autumn

Flowers in
Mid- to late summer

Perennial

RHS H5, USDA 5–10

This is a very tall allium with iridescent buds that open to near-spherical flowers. 'It works well with grasses and perennials,' says Eric Groft of Washington, DC-based landscape architects Oehme, van Sweden, for whom it is a signature plant. In his design for the American Museum Garden in Bath, southwest England, it threads between *Calamagrostis* x *acutiflora* 'Karl Foerster' (feather reed grass) and mustard-yellow *Rudbeckia fulgida* var. *sullivantii* 'Goldsturm' (rudbeckia), its elevated blooms lasting throughout summer. Later, the flowers evolve into round, bobbled seedheads.

In autumn, plant bulbs 15 cm (6 in) deep, in full sun, adding a handful of grit underneath each one to ensure they don't sit wet. After flowering, leave the foliage on the bulb to replenish its resources for the following summer.

Allium
sphaerocephalon

Allium

**Drumstick allium,
round-headed leek**

Syn. *Allium descendens*

Amaryllidaceae

Height
90 cm (35 in)

Position
Sun

Growing conditions
Any soil

Plant in
Early to late autumn

Flowers in
Mid- to late summer

Perennial

RHS H6, USDA 3–9

The flowers of *Allium sphaerocephalon* start green and so are camou-flaged among grasses until their pink colour drops down in summer, turning deeper red as the season progresses. Vertical in habit, this is a good companion for the spires of willow-leaved loosestrife (*Lysimachia ephemerum*) in a pairing that emphasizes the textural delicacy of its buds and flowers, offering a similar effect in a different shape. It is 'small, persistent and, most of all, late', notes Provence-based garden designer James Basson. With flowers that are among the smallest of all alliums, it is 'often used as a series of rhythmical dots to thread a garden together', says Katy Merrington, cultural gardener at the Hepworth Wakefield in Yorkshire, where it 'hovers among plants that by summer have finished flowering, to offer late colour'.

In autumn, plant bulbs 15 cm (6 in) deep, in sun or partial shade, adding a handful of grit and threading them in between existing plants. After flowering, leave the foliage on the bulbs to replenish them for the year ahead. They will increase underground, gradually forming clumps. This extremely long-flowering bulb really earns its keep.

Gladiolus papilio

Gladiolus

Butterfly sword lily

Iridaceae

Height
90 cm (35 in)

Position
Sun

Growing conditions
Warm, well-drained soil

Plant in
Early to late spring

Flowers in
Mid- to late summer

Perennial

RHS H4, USDA 6b–10

A less strident gladiolus with subtle beauty for a dry, sunny spot. The lilac flowers have pale yellow edges and are butter-yellow inside, marked with a bruised plum-coloured blotch. Native to South Africa, where it grows in damp, grassy places, it has flat, narrow foliage and widely spaced flowers that make it easy to combine with other plants. It looks lovely woven in small numbers through low-bunching grasses such as feather grass (*Stipa tenuissima*) and melic grass (*Melica altissima* 'Alba'), where its flowers do not register too heavily among their gossamer forms. Although the flowers do not open wide, this is a great bee plant, with enough room inside for a large foraging bumblebee.

    In spring, plant corms 15 cm (6 in) deep with their pointed ends up, adding a handful of grit around and underneath each one to ensure they don't sit wet.

Gladiolus 'Ruby'

Gladiolus

Sword lily

Syn. *Gladiolus papilio* 'Ruby'

Iridaceae

Height
75 cm (30 in)

Position
Sun

Growing conditions
Well-drained soil

Plant in
Late spring to early
summer

Flowers in
Mid- to late summer

Perennial

RHS H4, USDA 7–8

Gladiolus 'Ruby' combines the intense colour of a modern hybrid with the poise and ease of a species plant. The flowers are well spaced on their stems and held above flat, narrow foliage. Their rich red colour contrasts with darker markings inside the flowers to hypnotic effect. It threads easily between other summer-flowering perennials and is equally lovely planted in scant amounts through low-bunching grasses, such as melic grass (*Melica altissima* 'Alba'), where it hints at wild places.

In spring, plant corms 10 cm (4 in) deep where the flowers will catch the light when they open, adding a handful of grit with each one to ensure they don't sit wet. Leave the foliage in place after flowering to replenish numbers for the following year. Reliably perennial, it readily increases underground to gradually form clumps.

Lilium pardalinum var. giganteum

Lilium

Giant leopard lily

Liliaceae

Height
1.5 m (59 in)

Position
Sun or partial shade

Growing conditions
Any soil

Plant in
Early to mid-autumn
or early to mid-spring

Flowers in
Early to midsummer

Perennial

RHS H6, USDA 5–9

'The giant leopard lily of North America grows well above head height if it favours your ground,' says British garden designer Dan Pearson. 'Vividly scarlet with a splash of red exposed by flung-back petals, it has no perfume, but is easily forgiven for such ease and drama.' At Hillside, Pearson's private garden in the southwest of England, he grows it with magenta Armenian cranesbill (*Geranium psilostemon*) and lime-green spurge (*Euphorbia cornigera*) as part of a ripple of colourful planting close to the house. Atop narrow foliage, the red flowers are marked with dark spots.

Bulbs benefit from deep, rich soil and a cool root run. Plant them in spring, 15 cm (6 in) deep and no closer than 30 cm (12 in) to each other, with a handful of grit around each bulb.

Lilium pomponium

Lilium

Minor Turk's cap lily

Liliaceae

Height
70 cm (28 in)

Position
Partial shade

Growing conditions
Rich, deep soil that doesn't
lie wet

Plant in
Late winter to early spring

Flowers in
Midsummer

Perennial

RHS H6, USDA 4–8

Based in southern France, British garden designer James Basson is known for his expert knowledge of plants that are suited to the drier summers and wet but less cold winters many of us are experiencing as a result of climate change. *Lilium pomponium* is his lily of choice: a European native in a red that is 'extraordinarily elegant and almost brash', but with the elegance of a wildflower. The flowers number from two to seven per stem.

Plant bulbs shallowly in spring, the tip of each one a few centimetres (an inch or two) proud of the surface of the soil, in a position where the flowers will be in the sun when they open. *L. pomponium* needs very good drainage, so add a handful of grit under and around the bulb to ensure it doesn't sit wet. Not an easy plant for beginners, it is spectacularly rewarding.

Martagon lilies

Lilium
Liliaceae

Position
Dappled shade

Growing conditions
Rich, deep soil that doesn't
lie wet

Plant in
Late winter to early spring

Flowers in
Early to midsummer

Perennial

RHS H6, USDA 4–8

Woodlanders with well spaced flowers held in large numbers on their stems, martagon lily flowers turn upwards from dangling buds with their stamens pushing below. Their shape and spotted patterning give them the common name of 'Turk's cap lily'. Tall plants, they retain a degree of transparency and so are a useful upper storey to grasses and ferns in dappled shade. After six good weeks of blooming, the flowers evolve into polished and decorative seedheads that turn papery as the season progresses. *Lilium martagon* is 'happy to naturalize quietly, surviving in neglected gardens', says British designer Isabel Bannerman.

Plant bulbs in spring, 15 cm (6 in) deep in humus-rich soil, with a handful of grit around each one. Position them no closer than 30 cm (12 in) from each other to give the flowerheads space to breathe. In rough grass they readily self-seed, taking five years to reach flowering size. As with all lilies, keep an eye out for lily beetles, which are scarlet and black, very visible and must be picked off by hand.

Lilium martagon

Muted mauve-pink
flowers, darkly flecked,
with dark anthers.

Height 1.5 m (59 in)

**RHS Award of Garden Merit
(AGM)**

Lilium martagon 'Album'

White flowers that glow in dappled light and are 'lovely with all kinds of grasses', says Swedish landscape architect Ulf Nordfjell.

Height 1.5 m (59 in)

Lilium 'Arabian Knight'

Marmalade-coloured flowers, brown at the tips and flecked with brown spots.

Height 90 cm (35 in)

Lilium 'Claude Shride'

'Beautifully rich, deep flowers that contrast with taller grasses', notes British landscape designer Hugo Bugg. The dark red flowers are flecked with orange and have brown-orange anthers.

Height 1.5 m (59 in)

Lilium 'Sunny Morning'

Orange-yellow flowers heavily spotted with dark orange.

Height 90 cm (35 in)

Following pages:

With tall stems, green foliage and strongly recurved flowers, *Lilium martagon* 'Album' is useful for illuminating dappled shade

Giant-flowered lilies

Lilium
Liliaceae

Position
Sun

Growing conditions
Well-drained soil or gritty compost

Plant in
Early autumn to late spring

Flowers in
Midsummer

Perennial

RHS H6, USDA 4–8

Right:

Lilium 'African Queen'

Trumpet lily

Pink buds open to apricot-orange flowers with brownish-pink markings on the outer petals. Fragrant.

Height 1.5 m (59 in)

RHS Award of Garden Merit (AGM)

Opposite:

Lilium 'Conca d'Or'

Orienpet lily

Supersized white trumpet flowers with a lemon-yellow throat.

Height 1.4 m (55 in)

RHS Award of Garden Merit (AGM)

Gigantic trumpet lilies have become part of the lexicon of the modern English flower garden, used as part of an eclectic mix of annuals, perennials and woody plants in richly layered combinations. Their huge flowers have a Dixter-esque quality that taps into British eccentricity, offering a change of scale and shape in contrast, as seen in Malverleys garden in Hampshire and Wildside in Devon. The apricot-orange flowers of *Lilium* 'African Queen' are bright pink in bud and a good match for the pink summer flowers of smoke bush (*Cotinus coggygria*). Yellow mullein (*Verbascum chaixii*) and black-eyed Susan (*Rudbeckia fulgida* var. *sullivantii* 'Goldsturm') are beautifully countered by the boldness of *L.* 'Conca d'Or'.

The bulbs benefit from deep, rich soil and a cool root run. Ahead of planting, ensure they are out of the ground for as little time as possible, as they do not have a protective coat. In autumn, plant them 15 cm (6 in) deep, with a handful of grit under and around each bulb to deter slugs.

Lilium regale

Lilium

Regal lily, royal lily

Liliaceae

Height
1.5 m (59 in)

Position
Sun

Growing conditions
Well-drained soil or
gritty compost

Plant in
Early autumn to late
spring

Flowers in
Midsummer

Perennial

RHS H6, USDA 4–8

The white trumpet flowers of *Lilium regale* are beautifully marked
on the petal reverse in deep, rich plum, which is also present in the
bud, stem and foliage. This is a fantastic lily for pots and is often
grown next to a doorway to emphasize its heft and fragrance (use
a large pot to anchor it firmly and ensure it does not blow over).
'It's interesting to look at from the moment the first foliage erupts
on to the soil surface,' notes garden writer Kendra Wilson. 'The
flowers have stature, vitality (with the help of many different pollinators) and scent.'

In late spring, plant three bulbs per pot, 20 cm (8 in) deep, in
a gritty, loam-based mix, two parts compost to one part horticultural grit. The bulbs need plenty of compost below them and a cool
root run. Offer some shelter initially, as it shoots early and can be
damaged by frosts; then move it into its final spot in early summer.
Very perennial, it reaches full height – about 1–1.5 m (3–5 ft) –
from its second year in flower.

Tulbaghia violacea

Tulbaghia

Society garlic

Amaryllidaceae

Height
40 cm (16 in)

Position
Sun

Growing conditions
Well-drained soil

Plant in
Late spring to mid-autumn

Flowers in
Late spring to mid-autumn

Perennial

RHS H3, USDA 7b–10b

Society garlic has pink umbels of small flowers held in constellations from late spring until the first frosts. It is prolific and very long flowering, but the scale of the flowers and their distribution mean that it retains a feeling of lightness. The foliage is narrow, soft grey-green and grass-like, and the flowers are the tiniest bit recurved, like airy, miniature hyacinths. Its South African heritage belies a hardy nature and it is a good choice for a gravel or city garden with open, sunny conditions. It also grows well in a pot with minimal watering. At Le Jardin Secret in Marrakesh, Morocco, by British designer Tom Stuart-Smith, it is used under olive trees, threaded lightly among feather grass (*Stipa tenuissima*), rosemary and lavender; it illuminates the planting and appears to hover in low light.

    Tulbaghia violacea is typically offered for sale in pots in early summer. Plant it with a handful of grit around the roots to ensure it doesn't sit wet. Remove the spent flowers before they form seedpods to increase flowering further.

Tulbaghia violacea 'Silver Lace'

Tulbaghia

Society garlic

Amaryllidaceae

Height
40 cm (16 in)

Position
Sun

Growing conditions
Well-drained soil

Plant in
Late spring to mid-autumn

Flowers in
Late spring to mid-autumn

Perennial

RHS H3, USDA 7b–10b

RHS Award of Garden Merit (AGM)

Flowers at the violet end of the spectrum are at their best later in the day, when light levels drop, illuminating the gloaming. With pale flowers prettily marked with a deep pink central line and narrow, silver-edged, greyish-green foliage, the whole of *Tulbaghia violacea* 'Silver Lace' reflects the light. The flower stems are lax, so the flowers loll with grace and ease. The darker pink markings on the petals direct pollinators inside. A choice cultivar that is generous in its flowering, it deserves to be more popular.

Bulbs are typically offered in pots in early summer. Plant with a handful of grit around the root to avoid it sitting wet. Removing the spent flowers will encourage further flowering. Protect the plants from frost and keep in a sheltered position.

Liatris spicata 'Alba'

Liatris

Blazing star

Asteraceae

Height
90 cm (35 in)

Position
Sun or partial shade

Growing conditions
Well-drained soil

Plant in
Late spring to early summer

Flowers in
Midsummer to early autumn

Perennial

RHS H7, USDA 3–8

A delight in its mutability, the decorative, bobbled buds of *Liatris spicata* 'Alba' give way to narrow, bottlebrush-like flowers that are easy to use in a contemporary garden. Mid-height and with a narrow footprint, it is a useful vertical accent when the scale of a space is not suited to a very tall plant. At the Lurie Garden in Millennium Park, Chicago, by Dutch designer and plantsperson Piet Oudolf, it threads through *Echinacea*, *Eryngium*, *Amsonia* and wild quinine (*Parthenium integrifolium*) to make a beautiful textural combination, with architectural seedheads later in the year. A magnet for pollinators, its flowers are especially popular with smaller insects that will also overwinter in its hollow stems.

Plant corms 15 cm (6 in) deep in spring, with the smooth side down and adding a handful of grit underneath to ensure they don't sit wet.

Gladiolus 'Nathalie'

Gladiolus Nanus Group

Sword lily

Iridaceae

Height
70 cm (28 in)

Position
Sun

Growing conditions
Well-drained soil

Plant in
Late spring to early summer
at two-week intervals

Flowers in
Midsummer

Perennial

RHS H3, USDA 8–10

Traditional gladioli can be a challenge to integrate into the garden border, as their blooms are often brutish, brash and far removed from the simpler flower forms found in nature. By contrast, *Gladiolus* 'Nathalie' has toasted-pink flowers, flecked in apricot and darker at the tips. They open widely and are well spaced on their stems, making it easy to combine with other plants. A sweep of it among tall grasses is a wonderful thing. A small hybrid in the Nanus Group (the name means 'dwarf'), it also grows well in pots and is good as a cut flower.

In spring, plant corms 10 cm (4 in) deep where the flowers will be in sun when they open. Add a handful of grit with each corm to ensure they don't sit wet. Leave the foliage in place after flowering to replenish the corms for the following year. *G.* 'Nathalie' increases readily underground to gradually form a clump. To extend the flowering season, plant corms at fortnightly intervals from late spring.

Gladiolus murielae

Gladiolus

Abyssinian gladiolus

Syn. *Acidanthera murielae*

Iridaceae

Height
1 m (39 in)

Position
Sun

Growing conditions
Well-drained soil

Plant in
Early to late spring, protect
from frost

Flowers in
Late summer to mid-autumn

Tender perennial

RHS H3, USDA 8–10

**RHS Award of Garden Merit
(AGM)**

With white flowers marked with a star-shaped plum-coloured
blotch and held nimbly above tapering foliage, this delicate-
looking species gladiolus is bright and scented, especially late in
the day. Said to flower exactly 100 days from planting, its refined
colour palette and form are a refreshing counterpoint to the
larger, more richly hued flowers of summer. British designer Isabel
Bannerman notes that it is 'easy, inexpensive, reliable and beautiful'. It is best appreciated woven through gauzy, hummock-forming
grasses, where its shape is easy to read.

Start corms in pots of gritty compost before the last risk of
frost has passed. Plant one per pot, 15 cm (6 in) deep in a mix of two
parts loam-based compost to one part horticultural grit, and keep
in a sheltered position, ready to move into the garden later in spring.

Bessera elegans

Bessera

Coral drops

Asparagaceae

Height
70 cm (28 in)

Position
Sun

Growing conditions
Well-drained soil

Plant in
Mid-spring

Flowers in
Late summer to early autumn

Perennial

RHS H2, USDA 8–10

According to the American ceramicist and gardener Frances Palmer, *Bessera elegans* 'has wire-like stems that allow you to leave it at full length and use in large quantities in a vase with the flowers hovering on top'. Palmer limits the flowers she grows in her Connecticut garden to those she can cut and put in a vessel, and this is one of the best. Narrow grassy foliage gives way to brilliant scarlet flowers, striped white inside. Native to the scrub and grassy slopes of southwest and central Mexico, this is an elegant flower best grown in pots of gritty compost where corms can be sheltered from frosts.

    Plant corms 6 cm (2½ in) deep in a gritty mix, two parts loam-based compost to one part horticultural grit, in early spring. Move the pots outside as the weather warms. This is a good choice for a table top where the flowers can be observed at close quarters. After flowering and a dry winter rest, refresh the compost in spring.

Tritonia disticha subsp. *rubrolucens*

Tritonia

Pink montbretia

Syn. *Crocosmia rosea,
Tritonia rosea*

Iridaceae

Height
1 m (39 in)

Position
Sun

Growing conditions
Well-drained soil

Plant in
Mid-spring

Flowers in
Late summer to early autumn

Perennial

RHS H4, USDA 6b–10b

A lovely hazy, summer-flowering bulb that is hard to beat for a sunny spot, where its toasted-pink flowers appear to hover at mid-height. Tapering, vertical leaves push up ahead of long, narrow stems that eventually curve under the weight of their flowers. Native to South Africa, it is a good choice for a gravel, rubble or sand garden in combination with candelabra sage (*Salvia candelabrum*), vervain (*Verbena officinalis* var. *grandiflora* 'Bampton') and honeywort (*Cerinthe major* 'Purpurascens') as part of a muted and long-flowering palette. Alternatively, mix it with blue agapanthus and blue asters in a bolder combination. Easy to grow, it will overwinter in a sheltered spot.

     The corms benefit from a spadeful of compost as a winter mulch. In spring, plant them 10 cm (4 in) deep in a sunny situation, in clusters of three to five bulbs. Add a handful of grit around each one to ensure they don't sit wet.

Cardiocrinum cordatum var. *glehnii*

Cardiocrinum

Turep lily, Giant Japanese lily

Syn. *Lilium cordatum var. glehnii*

Liliaceae

Height
1.2 m (47 in)

Position
Dappled shade

Growing conditions
Damp, humus-rich soil

Plant in
Early to late spring

Flowers in
Late summer to early autumn

Monocarpic

RHS H5, USDA 6b–10

Tokachi Millennium Forest in Hokkaido, northern Japan, was designed by British garden designer Dan Pearson and is gardened by head gardener Midori Shintani, with the big idea that it should be sustainable for a thousand years. The giant Himalayan lily *Cardiocrinum cordatum var. glehnii* is a beautiful Hokkaido native that, grown from seed, takes more than seven years to reach flowering size and blooms only once. 'When I see its confetti-like seeds dancing in the wind I wish that it would continue forever,' says Shintani. A woodland plant for dappled shade, it earns its keep with a long stem and numerous heavy trumpet flowers, leavened by their greenish-white colour. Later, red-streaked seedpods reach skywards. A connoisseur's bulb for damp, woodsy soil, plant it in the company of deciduous and evergreen ferns.

Plant bulbs in spring, 15 cm (6 in) deep, with a handful of grit around each one to deter slugs. Keep bulbs no closer than 30 cm (12 in) to each other to give the flowers space to breathe.

Acis autumnalis

Acis

Autumn snowflake

Syn. *Leucojum autumnale*

Amaryllidaceae

Height
22 cm (7 in)

Position
Sun

Growing conditions
Sharp drainage

Plant in
Late summer

Flowers in
Late summer to early autumn

Perennial

RHS H5, USDA 7a–9

RHS Award of Garden Merit (AGM)

A lovely little perennial bulb that is easily overlooked on account of its small stature and delicate habit. The conical white flowers have a papery look to their petals, which are held in pretty relief atop narrow, vertical stems. Commonly known as the autumn snowflake, it grows in the wild in small groups in scrub and on rocky hillsides in the Mediterranean. The foliage disappears as the flowers arrive, making them more visible to pollinating insects. It's a good candidate for a pot alongside other late-flowering miniature treasures, such as *Erodium*. Designer Ron Lutsko, based in California, describes it as 'great for effortless, delicate fall flowers in the hot, dry season'.

The bulbs are small. In spring, plant them 8 cm (3 in) deep in clusters, almost touching each other, in pots, using one part horticultural grit to two parts compost. A further topping of grit will prevent the flower from getting dirtied when it rains.

Autumn & Early Winter

The expectation of late-flowering bulbs is welcome during a season of retreat, as shortening days mark a pivot in the gardening year. The quirky flowers of *Nerine bowdenii* are counterintuitive lipstick-pink, and valuable for that, appearing in autumn and ahead of their foliage, using the energy stored from a previous spring in leaf. As the ground becomes more visible, the perky flowers of *Cyclamen hederifolium* are triggered by the onset of wet weather. Useful for pollinators and easily spotted from on the wing above silvered foliage, they have a luminous quality and appear to hover in low light. The small flowers of *Colchicum* thrive in every kind of soil and will connect different parts of a garden. Famed for flowering precociously, even before the corm is planted, their tenacity is also legendary.

Around the winter solstice, when the ground is crunchy underfoot, jumbo-flowered *Hippeastrum* bulbs are easy to coax into early flower in the warmth of the house, offering a shot of vibrant colour. For a subtler display but an alluring scent, dainty paperwhites will flower at the same time. Outdoors, tucked under the frosty surface, triggered by autumn rain, snowdrop bulbs start to grow new roots, the beginnings of next year.

Nerine bowdenii

Nerine

Autumn lily, Bowden lily

Amaryllidaceae

Height
50 cm (20 in)

Position
Full sun

Growing conditions
Well-drained soil

Plant in
Summer

Flowers in
Early to late autumn

Perennial

RHS H5, USDA 7b–11

RHS Award of Garden
Merit (AGM)

A key autumn player that is well worth the wait for its curiously shaped, narrowly petalled pink flowers. It is described by British designer Sarah Price as 'a lily impersonator in lipstick pink, with a glittery sheen in the sun'. Native to the Drakensberg mountains of South Africa, where it grows in rocky ground, in the garden it is an uplifting sight against the browning foliage of autumn. Long flowering, the blooms appear on naked stems, ahead of their foliage. It is best grown where it is not overshadowed, since the bulbs must have a warm summer bake and will benefit from the reflected heat at the foot of a sunny wall.

In late summer, plant bulbs shallowly, one-third above, two-thirds below the soil, adding a handful of grit underneath and around each bulb. They can be shy to flower if planted too deeply, and it is not unusual for them to take up to two years to bloom.

Nerine for pots

Nerine

Autumn lily, Bowden lily

Amaryllidaceae

Position
Undercover

Growing conditions
Warm and bright

Plant in
Midsummer

Flowers in
Early to late autumn

Perennial

RHS H3, USDA 9a–10a

Most nerines are not hardy in a temperate climate and so are best grown indoors in pots as brilliant and easy-to-please houseplants. Flecked neon, mauve-striped, brightly coloured and tipped, the otherworldly flowers have immediate appeal, unfurling at a point in the year when colour is mostly in retreat. They are wonderful to grow in pots on a sunny windowsill as an eclectic mix of cultivars.

In summer, plant bulbs singly in vessels of a gritty mix – two parts loam-based compost to one part horticultural grit – choosing pots that are just a few centimetres (about an inch) wider than each bulb and keeping the top third of the bulb proud of the compost's surface. Stand pots in a warm, bright spot and water sparingly at first, then more regularly as the flowers appear. The flowers bloom ahead of their foliage and an extra layer of horticultural grit on top of the compost will keep watering to a minimum. After flowering, remove the seedpods so energy is directed back into the bulb to replenish and encourage flowering the following year. Keep on the dry side when dormant during summer.

Nerine 'Zeal Giant'

Syn. *Nerine bowdenii* 'Zeal Giant'

Dusky pink petals with a twist, darker at the tips.

Height 40 cm (16 in)

RHS Award of Garden Merit (AGM)

Nerine sarniensis 'Berlioz'

Narrowly petalled scarlet flowers with a darker central rib.

Height 40 cm (16 in)

Nerine sarniensis 'Dingan'

Narrow plum-coloured petals with paler plum markings.

Height 40 cm (16 in)

Nerine 'Hotspur'

Bright carmine flowers marked in purple. Later flowering than most nerines.

Height 40 cm (16 in)

Nerine sarniensis 'Quest'

Wide petals in dusty plum and pink.

Height 40 cm (16 in)

Cyclamen hederifolium

Cyclamen

Ivy-leafed cyclamen, Neapolitan cyclamen

Syn. *Cyclamen neapolitanum*

Primulaceae

Height
15 cm (6 in)

Position
Sun or partial shade

Growing conditions
Humus-rich soil that doesn't lie wet

Plant in
Early to mid-autumn

Flowers in
Mid- to late autumn

Perennial

RHS H5, USDA 5a–10

RHS Award of Garden Merit (AGM)

This lovely *Cyclamen* is set apart by its silver-marbled, green foliage that arrives as the flowers fade (*hedera* translates from Latin as 'ivy', so the species name means 'ivy leaved'). The flowers have a light-giving quality and are prettily reflexed, rising nimbly on narrow stems, their opening timed to coincide with the onset of winter wet. It is happy growing in full or dappled shade, in dry or damp soil, so it is useful for connecting different parts of a garden: grow it in gravel, in grass, at the front of a border or in the rooty places under decid- uous trees and shrubs. 'It is great under native oaks, where it seeds around to make delightful colonies,' says the American landscape architect Ron Lutsko. British designer Sarah Price also grows it in this way, in a single-species sweep alongside deciduous ferns.

The tubers are round and flat. Plant them 5 cm (2 in) deep in humus-rich soil in autumn, just as they start into growth. Tiny, juve- nile flowering shoots on the top of the tuber indicate the right way up. Water once on planting, if the weather is dry; they shouldn't need watering after that. Add a mulch of leaf litter on top of the soil in spring as the foliage disappears.

Colchicum autumnale

Colchicum

Autumn crocus, meadow saffron

Syn. *Colchicum autumnale* 'Wild Form'

Colchicaceae

Height
15 cm (6 in)

Position
Sun or partial shade

Growing conditions
Any soil

Plant in
Late spring to early summer

Flowers in
Early to mid-autumn

Perennial

RHS H5, USDA 4a–8b

RHS Award of Garden Merit (AGM)

The small flowers of autumn crocus are easy to read, being among the very few to appear at this particular moment in the year. A wood-lander, *Colchicum autumnale* could not be easier to grow and is famed for flowering even before the corm is planted. The flowers are sturdy and resilient in inclement weather, with a luminous quality that makes them appear to glow in low light. This is a useful little plant for connecting different parts of the garden, including under deciduous trees and shrubs; in grass, it will take advantage of the gap in mowing to replenish its energy after flowering. It is dormant in summer.

Plant corms 8 cm (3 in) deep, 15 cm (6 in) apart in late spring or early summer, using a trowel or hori hori to make slots in the soil. Add a mulch of leaf litter in spring as the foliage disappears.

Crocus pulchellus

Crocus

**Hairy crocus,
Mount Athos crocus**

Iridaceae

Height
10 cm (4 in)

Position
Sun or partial shade

Growing conditions
Any soil

Plant in
Mid- to late autumn

Flowers in
Mid-autumn to early winter

Perennial

RHS H6, USDA 5–9

**RHS Award of Garden Merit
(AGM)**

A spirited little flower that is triggered into growth by dropping temperatures and the onset of wet weather. The small flowers (pictured here planted with heuchera) appear ahead of short, narrow, grass-like foliage and are more deeply coloured on the petal reverse. Mat Reese, head gardener at Malverleys garden in Hampshire, says: 'Every October it always comes as a bit of a surprise to have *Crocus pulchellus* pushing up a host of delicate, pearl-blue flowers when much of the garden is on the ebb. The blooms are decorated on the inside with attractive darker filigree veining, a showy orange stigma, and a yellow throat. It grows well on the terrace at Malverleys in gravelly soil and makes small, slowly expanding colonies which the field mice tend to keep in check.' *C. pulchellus* is best grown en masse as a single-species sweep. Dependable and, for a crocus, early flowering, it is a useful source of pollen at a time of year when forage is becoming scarce.

Position the corms where the low winter sun will hit the ground as the flowers open, as they close up on overcast days when fewer pollinators fly. In autumn, plant 7 cm (3 in) deep, 5 cm (2 in) apart, with the pointed ends up, using a trowel or hori hori to make slots in the soil and dropping the corms in.

Narcissus papyraceus 'Ziva'

Narcissus

Paperwhite daffodil

Syn. *Narcissus tazetta* subsp. *papyraceus*

Amaryllidaceae

Height
45 cm (18 in)

Position
Indoors

Growing conditions
Cool and bright

Plant in
Early winter

Flowers in
Midwinter

Annual

RHS H4, USDA 9–11

Commonly known as paperwhites, *Narcissus papyraceus* 'Ziva' is a bunch-flowering daffodil whose small white flowers offer a heady scent. Popularly 'forced' indoors to flower in time for Christmas, it is the most highly scented of all the narcissus. Bulbs sold as 'prepared' have been stored at low temperatures for several weeks prior to sale so that they flower swiftly once planted, triggered by light and warmth.

To force paperwhites into early flowering, plant 10–15 per pot, 2.5 cm (1 in) apart in a gritty mix, two parts loam-based compost to one part horticultural grit. The pointed end of each bulb should just nudge the surface. Keep the pot in a cool spot until the bulbs start to shoot, then move it into the warmth; provide support using a scaffold of twiggy branches from the garden, as the flowers are heavy for their stems. Topping the compost with a layer of sustainably sourced moss makes a magical table-piece.

Hippeastrum
(Spider Group)
'Bogota'

Hippeastrum

Amaryllis

Amaryllidaceae

Height
45 cm (18 in)

Position
Indoors

Growing conditions
Warm and bright

Plant in
Mid- to late autumn

Flowers in
Midwinter

Annual

RHS H2, USDA 9–11

A treat of a bulb for forcing during the dark days of winter, with narrow scarlet flowers, dark in the middle and with a hint of red in the bud, stem and foliage. In common with others in its family, the flowers open before the foliage.

To force the bulb to flower indoors in winter, plant in a pot that is only a few centimetres (an inch or so) wider than the bulb in gritty compost, keeping the top two-thirds of the bulb proud of the surface. Stand the pot in the warmth and light, watering sparingly, then regularly when the first shoots push up. It will flower six weeks after planting. The flowering stems have a tendency to lean towards the light, which can be countered by giving the pot a quarter-turn every few days.

Hippeastrum
(Galaxy Group)
'Christmas Gift'

Hippeastrum

Amaryllis

Amaryllidaceae

Height
45 cm (18 in)

Position
Indoors

Growing conditions
Warm and bright

Plant in
Mid- to late autumn

Flowers in
Midwinter

Annual

RHS H2, USDA 9–11

The array of amaryllis bulbs on offer is a consequence of over 220 years of breeding work, predominantly in search of bigger and blowsier flowers. The trumpets of *Hippeastrum* 'Christmas Gift' are gratifyingly jumbo-sized but, white with pale green throats, they are leavened by their colour.

Plant one bulb per pot, into a pot that is only a few centimetres (an inch or so) wider than the bulb, filled almost to the lip with gritty compost. Leave the top two-thirds of the bulb proud of the soil. Keep it warm indoors and water sparingly until the shoots push up, then more often as the flowers open. Bulbs flower 7–10 weeks after planting. The flowering stems have a tendency to lean towards the light, which can be countered by giving the pot a quarter-turn every few days. As the flower is heavy, the stem benefits from the support of a branch cut from the garden.

Hippeastrum
'Terra Mystica'

Hippeastrum

Amaryllis

Amaryllidaceae

Height
45 cm (18 in)

Position
Indoors

Growing conditions
Warm and bright

Plant in
Mid- to late autumn

Flowers in
Midwinter

Annual

RHS H2, USDA 9–11

Hippeastrum 'Terra Mystica' is a standout favourite, for its height and slightly smaller flowers. While many *Hippeastrum* flowers are heavy for their stems and need support to counter their weight, this one's single flowers remain upright. Muted orange with a darker throat, they are beautifully coloured.

To force the bulb to flower indoors in winter, plant in gritty compost in a pot that is only a few centimetres (an inch or so) wider than the bulb, keeping the top two-thirds of the bulb proud of the surface. Stand the pot in the warmth and light and water sparingly, then regularly when the first shoots push up. It will flower six weeks after planting. The flowering stems have a tendency to lean towards the light, which can be countered by giving the pot a quarter-turn every few days.

Hippeastrum papilio

Hippeastrum

Amaryllis

Amaryllidaceae

Height
45 cm (18 in)

Position
Indoors

Growing conditions
Warm and bright

Plant in
Mid- to late autumn

Flowers in
Midwinter

Annual

RHS H2, USDA 9–11

A kitsch, chunkily flowered amaryllis, intricately marked in green, white and plum, the colours of winter-mix sweets. While many *Hippeastrum* are heavy for their stems and need support to counter the weight of their flowers, this one is shorter stemmed than most and stands without support.

To force the bulb to flower indoors in winter, plant it in a pot that is only a few centimetres (an inch or so) wider than the bulb. Use a gritty compost, keeping the top two-thirds of the bulb proud of the surface. Stand the pot in the warmth and light and water sparingly, then regularly when the first shoots push up, but never allowing the bulb to sit wet. Bulbs flower 7–10 weeks after planting. The flowering stems have a tendency to lean towards the light, which can be countered by giving the pot a quarter-turn every few days.

Hippeastrum
(Colibri Group)
'Rapido'

Hippeastrum

Amaryllis

Amaryllidaceae

Height
45 cm (18 in)

Position
Indoors

Growing conditions
Warm and bright

Plant in
Mid- to late autumn

Flowers in
Midwinter

Annual

RHS H3, USDA 9–11

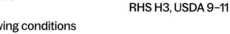

The drawback of planting winter-flowering bulbs in late summer is that at the time of choosing which bulbs to plant, we are just emerging from months of saturated colour. It is all too easy to go for the more subtle shades, only to find later that we are in want of a bigger hit of colour. *Hippeastrum* 'Rapido' is smaller flowered than most, with a graceful habit but electrifying colour. Its jolting red trumpets are more deeply red inside. It will flower for up to four weeks in a cool spot indoors. While many *hippeastrum* flowers are heavy for their stems and need support to counter their weight, the dainty, single flowers of 'Rapido' are not too far removed from the species form and remain upright.

To force the bulbs into winter flowering, plant them individually into pots of a gritty mix, two parts loam-based compost to one part horticultural grit, keeping the top two-thirds of the bulb proud of the surface of the compost. Keep them in the warmth and light, watering sparingly and then regularly as the flowers open. The stems have a tendency to lean towards the light, which can be countered by giving the pot a quarter-turn every few days.

Bulbs by Use

Useful for pollinators

Allium angulosum
Allium 'Mont Blanc'
Allium siculum
Allium sphaerocephalon
Allium tripedale
Crocus pulchellus
Cyclamen hederifolium
Fritillaria imperialis
Fritillaria meleagris
Gladiolus 'Nathalie'
Gladiolus papilio
Ipheion sp.
Liatris spicata 'Alba'
Nerine bowdenii
Ornithogalum umbellatum
Species tulips
Tulbaghia violacea
Tulbaghia violacea
 'Silver Lace'
Tulipa 'Lady Jane'

Architectural seedheads

Allium angulosum
Allium 'Pink Jewel'
Allium schubertii
Liatris spicata 'Alba'
Lilium martagon
Muscari armeniacum
Tulipa 'Lady Jane'

For scent

Galanthus 'Seagull'
Hyacinthus orientalis
 'Anastasia'
Hyacinthus orientalis
 'Woodstock'
Iris 'Benton Nigel'
Iris reticulata 'Scent Sational'
Lilium 'African Queen'
Lilium regale
Muscari macrocarpum
 'Golden Fragrance'
Narcissus 'Falconet'
Narcissus fernandesii var.

 cordubensis
Narcissus papyraceus 'Ziva'
Narcissus poeticus
 'Recurvus'
Narcissus tazetta
Narcissus 'White Lady'

For containers

Anemone coronaria
 'Bordeaux'
Gladiolus murielae
Lilium regale
Nerine sp.
Ornithogalum ponticum
 'Sochi'
Scilla peruviana
Tulipa sp.

For smaller pots

Acis autumnalis
Fritillaria acmopetala
Fritillaria michailovski
Fritillaria uva-vulpis
Galanthus sp. (virescent and
 green snowdrops)
Iris reticulata
Muscari sp.
Narcissus bulbocodium
Scilla mischtschenkoana
 'Tubergeniana'
Species tulips

For naturalizing

Anemone blanda
Crocus pulchellus
Cyclamen hederifolium
Cyclamen repandum
Eranthis hyemalis
Erythronium californicum
Erythronium 'Joanna'
Erythronium 'Pagoda'
Galanthus elwesii
Galanthus nivalis
Gladiolus communis subsp.
 byzantinus

Muscari sp.
Narcissus sp.
Ornithogalum umbellatum
Trillium kurabayashii

For shady spots

Anemone nemorosa
 'Robinsoniana'
Colchicum autumnale
Cyclamen hederifolium
Erythronium californicum
Erythronium 'Joanna'
Erythronium 'Pagoda'
Ornithogalum pyrenaicum
Trillium kurabayashii
Tulipa sylvestris

Tall plants (over 1 m/3 ft)

Allium 'Mont Blanc'
Allium tripedale
Fritillaria imperialis
Fritillaria persica
Gladiolus murielae
Lilium pardalinum var.
 giganteum
Lilium regale
Tritonia disticha subsp.
 rubrolucens

For grass/turf

Camassia leichtlinii
Crocus 'Prins Claus'
Crocus tommasinianus
Crocus versicolor
Fritillaria meleagris
Galanthus nivalis
Gladiolus communis subsp.
 byzantinus
Leucojum aestivum
Leucojum aestivum
 'Gravetye Giant'
Lilium martagon
Narcissus sp.
Ornithogalum umbellatum
Puschkinia scilloides var.

 libanotica
Scilla bifolia
Tulipa sp.

For cut flowers

Fritillaria uva-vulpis
Gladiolus 'Nathalie'
Lilium regale
Narcissus tazetta
Nerine bowdenii
Ornithogalum ponticum
 'Sochi'
Tulipa sp.

For forcing

Anemone coronaria
 'Bordeaux'
Fritillaria uva-vulpis
Hippeastrum sp.
Narcissus bulbocodium
Narcissus papyraceus 'Ziva'

Practical Information

Bulb essentials

Bulbs have different requirements depending on their native habitat, but most grow best in sunny conditions in moisture-retentive, well-drained soil.

When buying bulbs, choose those that are firm and round, pressing them gently at the base to check their firmness.

A big bulb will flower better than a small bulb of the same type.

Plant flowering bulbs while they are dormant. Spring-flowering bulbs must be planted in autumn, summer-flowering bulbs in late spring, and autumn/winter-flowering bulbs in late summer.

Plant bulbs immediately after buying them. If this isn't possible, keep them cool, dry and away from direct sunlight.

Generally, plant bulbs with their pointed ends up, at a depth that is triple the height of the bulb.

Plant rhizomes horizontally.

Some bulbs, including nerines and hippeastrums, should be planted with the top third of the bulb above the surface of the soil.

After planting, water bulbs once to settle them into the soil. Bulbs in containers should be watered regularly when the flower buds appear.

Be aware that lily pollen is poisonous to cats.

How many to plant

Some bulbs need more space than others. Here is a guide to the average number to plant per square metre (1 m x 1 m) in soil or grass. For how many to plant to a square foot (1 ft x 1 ft), divide these figures by 10.

Allium
small (*angulosum, atropurpureum, sphaerocephalon*) → 20

large (*nigrum, obliquum, schubertii, siculum, tripedale*) → 15

Camassia → 10

Crocus, Galanthus, Leucojum, Muscari, Puschkinia, species tulips → 50

Narcissus, Tulipa → 30

Scilla
small (*bifolia, mischtschenkoana*) → 20

large (*hyacinthoides*) → 3

Fritillaria
small (*acmopetala, meleagris, michailovskyi, uva-vulpis*) → 15

large (*imperialis, persica*) → 5

Erythronium, Ipheion, Trillium → 5

Anemone, Cyclamen → 10

Sustainability

Buy bulbs that are packaged in paper or 100 per cent biodegradable packaging rather than in plastic nets.

Boost biodiversity in the garden by planting bulbs that flower early or late in the year when pollen and nectar are in short supply.

Choose organic bulbs where possible. The phosphate fertilizers, fungicides, pesticides and herbicides used in the production of non-organic bulbs can persist in the soil and flowers and leach into soil water, adversely affecting soil-dwelling creatures, mycorrhiza and pollinators.

Choose perennial bulbs rather than hybrids that have been bred to flower for just one year before they need to be replaced. Post-flower, leave the foliage in place for a minimum of six weeks to replenish resources; snap off seedpods to divert energy back into the bulb. Remove the spent petals of tulips, which can increase the risk of fungal diseases, such as tulip fire.

Trouble-shooting

No flowers

Bulbs that increase in number under the soil can stop flowering as competition between them for nutrients and water increases. Dividing a clump by separating it into individual bulbs and giving each one space to grow will reinvigorate flowering. Lift the whole clump of bulbs from the soil, separate it into single bulbs and replant them, spacing them widely apart and at the same depth as they were growing in the original clump. Gently firm in and water to settle them into the soil.

Disappearing bulbs

Bulbs that sit wet will rot away. To ensure this doesn't happen, add a handful of horticultural grit to their planting holes, particularly in heavier soil. Deter hungry mice, voles, squirrels and birds from digging up recently planted bulbs by putting holly sprigs on top of the soil or pots, or by covering pots with chicken wire for protection. Bulbs in the Liliaceae family (which includes tulips as well as lilies) can be prone to slug damage because they have no papery tunic to protect them. Add horticultural grit under, around and on top of the bulbs as you plant them.

Glossary

Disappearing leaves and flowers

The scarlet-and-black lily beetle and its larvae voraciously eat the leaves of lilies and fritillaries. The adult beetle is very visible and must be picked off by hand.

Tulip fire

This is a fungal disease that makes blotches on a tulip's leaves, distorts the growth of both flowers and leaves, and can eventually destroy the bulb. Plant bulbs in bright, sunny, well-drained conditions to reduce the humidity the fungus needs; if your bulbs are affected, grow tulips in a different spot for a minimum of three years.

Annual
A plant that completes its lifecycle in one year.

Bulb
A small bud on a round, flattened underground stem, surrounded by scale leaves; it stores water and food reserves for the next season in the swollen bases of its spent leaves.

Clump
A number of bulbs (or plants) growing closely together.

Corm
A swollen underground stem surrounded by a papery case which stores water and food reserves for the next flowering season. Buds on top of the corm grow into flowering stems and adventitious roots grow from the base. The corm is used up when it flowers and new corms form from it each year.

Floret
A small individual flower that is a component of a bigger flowerhead.

Forcing
Encouraging a plant to flower early by mimicking the cold, dark conditions of winter.

Hori hori
A Japanese trowel useful for planting bulbs.

Horticultural grit
Washed grit, with particles usually up to 5 mm (⅕ in) across, added to compost or soil to increase drainage.

'In the green'
A method of planting bulbs after they have finished flowering but while they still have their foliage attached.

Monocarpic
A plant that flowers once and then dies.

Naturalizing
Leaving bulbs underground after flowering so that they propagate themselves.

Perennial
A plant that repeats its lifecycle every twelve months.

Photosynthesis
The process by which plants use sunlight, water and carbon dioxide to make oxygen and energy.

Reflexed
Literally 'turning backwards' – used to describe petals or foliage that turn backwards.

Rhizome
A horizontal underground stem surrounded by a papery case which stores water and food reserves. In common with all stems, it has buds spaced along it that grow into leaves and flowering shoots.

Tuber
A swollen, underground stem or root that stores water and food reserves.

Umbel
A flower shape (inflorescence) in which flower stalks of equal length grow from a common centre to form a curved shape.

Suppliers

Ordering bulbs online offers the widest choice, and suppliers will send out bulbs at the correct time of year for planting them. Many nurseries allow you to place your order throughout the year. Otherwise, it is a good idea to sign up to mailing lists to be notified when the new season's offerings are available. Popular bulbs can sell out quickly.

FRANCE

Ernest Turc
ernest-turc.com
Bulb manufacturer and creator, Ernest Turc provides a range of high-quality bulbs and seeds. For five generations, it has built a solid reputation based on reliability and trust (with its customers).

Promesses de Fleurs
promessedefleurs.com
An extensive catalogue of bulbs and plants, with specific explanations and detailed advice on their culture. Shipping is fast and Europe-wide.

NETHERLANDS

Dutch Grown
dutchgrown.co.uk
Lesser-known and well-established favourites from a fourth-generation Dutch family bulb farm. A well-chosen selection includes narcissi, tulips, crocuses and alliums as well as lesser-known bulbs such as *Dichelostemma*.

Natural Bulbs
naturalbulbs.nl
A good selection of spring-flowering bulbs, with an emphasis on those for naturalizing, supplied by a small group of organic growers.

Nijssen Garden and Bulbs
nijssenbulbs.com
Well-established Dutch nursery and bulb supplier offering an extensive selection that includes historic bulbs and British snowdrop cultivars, with an emphasis on sustainable, chemical-free cultivation.

UK

Bloms bulbs
blomsbulbs.com
With a heritage of over 160 years, this award-winning nursery offers an extensive range of interesting bulbs supplied by British and Dutch growers.

Farmer Gracy
farmergracy.co.uk
Online nursery specializing in bulbs, with an extensive range for sale, including bulbs for pots, shade and pollinators. All bulbs are dispatched in paper packaging.

Jacques Amand
jacquesamandintl.com
Offers a wide selection of well-chosen bulbs, including species and historic tulips.

Organic Bulbs
organicbulbs.com
Landscape architects Lulu Urquhart and Adam Hunt's ecologically friendly bulb nursery, with an emphasis on bulbs for naturalizing and that benefit pollinators. All bulbs offered are chemical free.

Peter Nyssen
peternyssen.com
A well-established bulb nursery with over 50 years of Dutch heritage, offering an interesting selection bulbs year round to novice or more experienced gardeners. Delivers to the UK and EU.

Sarah Raven
sarahraven.co.uk
Offers an extensive range of bulbs alongside other garden-worthy plants. Sarah Raven's interest lies primarily in colourful combinations and new bulbs are added to the list each year to reflect current trends. The garden in East Sussex is open to visitors in spring and autumn to coincide with the peaks of the bulb displays.

Scamp's Daffodils
qualitydaffodils.com
Award-winning Cornwall-based nursery, notable for its specialist range of narcissi. The choice of bulbs is huge, with a stock list that includes over 2,500 varieties. The website is an excellent source of expert advice.

USA

Brent & Becky's
brentandbeckysbulbs.com
Established in 1900, this Virginia-based bulb nursery offers a wide selection of sustainably grown bulbs from its 28-acre (11-hectare) family farm. There is particular emphasis on narcissi, as well as a choice selection of the more usual bulbs.

John Scheepers
johnscheepers.com
Connecticut-based nursery offering an extensive range of bulbs for every season, including alliums, anemones, erythroniums and fritillaries.

Old House Gardens
oldhousegardens.com
Online heritage/heirloom bulb specialist, shipping throughout the USA.

Roozengaarde
tulips.com
Specialists in unusual narcissus, tulip and iris cultivars alongside more usual bulbs. Ships throughout the USA and Canada.

Index

Page numbers in *italics* refer to illustrations

List of Nominators

Paul Bangay
Garden designer,
Victoria, Australia

Isabel Bannerman
Garden designer,
Somerset, UK

James Basson
Garden designer,
Alpes-Maritimes, France

Conrad Batten
Garden designer/AMELD
Devon, UK

Anna Benn
Garden designer,
Oxford, UK

Jimi Blake
Gardener, Hunting Brook,
Co. Wicklow, Ireland

Valerie Bond
Garden and landscape
designer, and Associate
garden designer at Urquhart
& Hunt, Cork, Ireland, and
Somerset, UK

Marian Boswall
Landscape architect,
Kent, UK

Jonny Bruce
Plantsperson and
gardener, UK

Hugo Bugg
Landscape designer,
co-founder Harris Bugg
Studio, London, Exeter and
Isle of Skye, UK

Matt Collins
Head gardener,
Garden Museum,
London, UK

Tom Coward
Head gardener,
Gravetye Manor,
West Sussex, UK

Nigel Dunnett
Planting designer,
South Yorkshire, UK

Rory Dusoir
Gardener, garden designer
and writer, London, UK

Kimberly Fleming
Flower farmer and former
White House florist
under President Obama,
Berkshire, UK

Alys Fowler
Gardener and writer,
mid-Wales, UK

Fergus Garrett
Head gardener, Great Dixter
House & Garden,
East Sussex, UK

Eric Groft
CEO and Director,
Oehme van Sweden/OvS,
Washington, DC, USA

Charlie Harpur
Head gardener,
Knepp Castle Estate,
West Sussex, UK

Charlie Hawkes
Landscape designer,
Wiltshire, UK

Chris Ireland-Jones
Nurseryperson, formerly
of Avon Bulbs, Somerset, UK

Alison Jenkins
Regenerative gardener, UK

Mary Keen
Garden designer and writer,
Gloucestershire, UK

Noel Kingsbury
Plantsperson and educator,
Portugal and UK

Jacqueline van der Kloet
Garden designer and
planting specialist,
Weesp, Netherlands

Hans Kramer
Nurseryperson,
De Hessenhof, Netherlands

Ron Lutsko
Garden designer,
California, USA

James McGrath
Head gardener, Robin Hill,
Connecticut, USA

Manoj Malde
Garden designer, presenter
and author, London, UK

Fernando Martos
Landscape designer,
Madrid, Spain

Katy Merrington
Cultural gardener,
The Hepworth Wakefield,
West Yorkshire, UK

Ulf Nordfjell
Landscape architect,
Stockholm, Sweden

Martin Ogle
Garden and planting
designer, Cumbria, UK

Piet Oudolf
Landscape and garden
designer, Hummelo,
Netherlands

Frances Palmer
Ceramicist and gardener,
Connecticut, USA

Arthur Parkinson
Writer, gardener and
illustrator, UK

Dan Pearson
Landscape designer, London
and Somerset, UK

Sarah Price
Garden designer,
Monmouthshire, UK

Matthew Reese
Head gardener, Malverleys
garden, Hampshire, UK

Margaret Roach
Gardener, writer, columnist
for *The New York Times* and
host of the podcast 'A Way to
Garden', New York, USA

Cassian Schmidt
Landscape designer,
Hermannshof, Germany

Troy Scott Smith
Head gardener, Sissinghurst
Castle Garden, Kent, UK

Joe Sharman
Nurseryperson, Monksilver
Nursery, Cambridge, UK

Midori Shintani
Head gardener,
Tokachi Millennium Forest,
Hokkaido, Japan

R. William Thomas
Executive director,
Chanticleer, Wayne,
Pennsylvania, USA

Bernard Trainor
Ground Studio /
Landscape Architecture
California, USA

Miguel Urquijo
Landscape designer,
Urquijo-Kastner,
Madrid, Spain

Cleve West
Landscape designer,
London, UK

Kendra Wilson
Garden writer, UK and USA

Further Reading & Acknowledgements

Bellamy, Lucy. *Brilliant and Wild: A Garden from Scratch in a Year*. London: Pimpernel Press, 2018.

Bellamy, Lucy. *Grow 5: Simple Seasonal Recipes for Small Outdoor Spaces with Just Five Plants*. London: Mitchell Beazley, 2022.

Hessayon, Dr D. G. *The Bulb Expert: The World's Bestselling Book on Bulbs*. Totnes, Devon: Expert Books, 1995.

Kloet, Jacqueline van der. *Growing Bulbs in the Natural Garden: Innovative Techniques for Combining Bulbs and Perennials in Every Season*. Portland, Oregon: Timber Press, 2024.

Nicholson, Polly. *The Tulip Garden: Growing and Collecting Species, Rare and Annual Varieties*. London: Phaidon Press, 2024.

Pavord, Anna. *Bulb*. London: Mitchell Beazley, 2009.

Pavord, Anna. *The Seasonal Gardener: Creative Planting Combinations*. London: Phaidon Press, 2022.

Wilford, Richard. *The Kew Gardener's Companion to Growing Bulbs*. London: Kew Royal Botanic Gardens, 2019.

We would like to thank all the garden designers, writers, plantspeople and head gardeners who kindly shared their expertise and nominations for bulbs as we embarked on the making of this book. Their input and insight was invaluable. A special mention and thank you is due to Chris Ireland-Jones and Alan Street (who sadly passed away in 2022) of Avon Bulbs, who were both so generous with their time and knowledge, also allowing us access to the nursery to photograph many of the bulbs featured within these pages. In addition, thanks to Matthew Pottage, former curator at the RHS Garden Wisley, for giving us access to many of the RHS's bulb collections. Thank you to Sarah Brooks and Teresa Clements of the Wakefield and North of England Tulip Society for checking the English Florists' tulips pages, and to Eric Hsu of Chanticleer and botanist and plant collector Dr James Compton, both of whom checked the plant names and text at an early stage and gave feedback. We'd also like to thank the Society of Authors for their award of an Author's Foundation Grant. Last but not least, we would like to thank all the garden owners and gardens who gave access for photography:

Allt-y-Bela; Avon Bulbs; Belcombe Court; Benton End; Benton Iris Collection Garden; Blacklands; Blue Sky Botanics; Bob Brown; Bob Purnell; Caisson Gardens; Colebrook House; Colesbourne Gardens; Downtown House; East Lambrook Manor Gardens; Gravetye Manor; Gresgarth Hall; Hampton Court; Hanham Court Gardens; Hauser & Wirth Somerset; Hillier; Hortus Bulborum; Hunting Brook Gardens; Malverleys Garden; Mary Keen; Melplash Court; Morlas Plants; Old Court Nurseries and The Picton Garden; Orchard Dene; Parham Gardens; Phoenix Plants; Royal Horticultural Society; Sissinghurst Castle Garden; Special Plants Nursery; The Hepworth Wakefield; Ulf Nordfjell; Upton Wold; and Wildside.

– Lucy Bellamy and Jason Ingram

In addition, the publisher would like to thank the following for their editorial assistance: Caitlin Arnell Argles, Vanessa Bell, Rosie Fairhead, Diane Fortenberry, Tracey Smith and Caroline Taggart.

Phaidon Press Limited
2 Cooperage Yard
London E15 2QR

Phaidon Press Inc.
111 Broadway
New York, NY 10006

phaidon.com

First published 2024
© 2024 Phaidon Press Limited

ISBN 978 1 83866 846 4

A CIP catalogue record for this book is
available from the British Library and
the Library of Congress.

The publisher would like to thank the following
for the use of their images: Alamy Stock Photo:
George Ostertag 126; © Richard Bloom: 36, 67;
© Jonathan Buckley: 90, 146; Gap Photos:
Vision 58, Tim Gainey 59, 138, Joanna Kossak
61tr, Heather Edwards 116, Visions Premium 145,
Lynn Keddie 180; MMGI/Marianne Majerus:
95tm, 160; Reproduced by kind permission of the
National Trust: 79, 92–3; The Garden Collection/
FP: Andrew Lawson 176, Christine Ann Foll 193. All
other photographs are by Jason Ingram.

Commissioning Editor: Victoria Clarke
Project Editor: Victoria Clarke
Editorial Assistant: Caitlin Arnell Argles
Production Controller: Gif Jittiwutikarn

Designed by Associate

Printed in China

Editorial Note

The bulbs in this book are organized in four
seasonal chapters and they are sequenced
according to their flowering time, based on
a northern-hemisphere temperate climate.
Approximate flowering months are given in
each entry and are listed below, but these will
vary according to where you live.

The hardiness ratings given for each of the featured plants are based on Royal Horticultural
Society (RHS) recommendations in the UK
and USDA (United States Department of
Agriculture) ratings in the USA. Key dates are
included as a guide. You may need to adapt
these, and flowering times may also vary,
depending on where you live. RHS AGM details
are correct as of February 2024.

Seasons

In a northern-hemisphere temperate climate
the seasons translate as follows:

Midwinter	January
Late winter	February
Early spring	March
Mid-spring	April
Late spring	May
Early summer	June
Midsummer	July
Late summer	August
Early autumn	September
Mid-autumn	October
Late autumn	November
Early winter	December

RHS Award of Garden Merit (AGM)

The AGM award is given by the Royal
Horticultural Society (UK) to plants that
perform reliably, with the aim of helping
gardeners to choose the best plants for their
garden. An AGM award indicates that the
plant is excellent for ordinary use in the
appropriate conditions, is readily available,
has a good constitution, is stable in form
and colour and is reasonably resistant to
pests and diseases.